LIFE COMES FROM LIFE

BOOKS by His Divine Grace A.C. Bhaktivedanta Swami Prabhupada

Bhagavad-gītā As It Is
Śrīmad-Bhāgavatam, Cantos 1-12 (18 volumes)
Śrī Caitanya-caritāmṛta (17 volumes)
Teachings of Lord Kapila, the Son of Devahūti
Teachings of Lord Caitanya
Teachings of Queen Kuntī
The Nectar of Devotion
The Science of Self-Realization
The Journey of Self-Discovery
Kṛṣṇa, the Supreme Personality of Godhead (2 vols)
The Nectar of Instruction
Śrī Īśopaniṣad
Easy Journey to Other Planets
Kṛṣṇa Consciousness: The Topmost Yoga System
Perfect Questions, Perfect Answers
Kṛṣṇa, the Reservoir of Pleasure
The Path of Perfection
Life Comes from Life
The Perfection of Yoga
Beyond Birth and Death
On the Way to Kṛṣṇa
Rājā-vidya: The King of Knowledge
Elevation to Kṛṣṇa Consciousness
Kṛṣṇa Consciousness: The Matchless Gift
Geetār-gan (Bengali)
Vairāgya-vidya (Bengali)
Buddhi-yoga (Bengali)
Bhakti-ratna-bolī (Bengali)
Back to Godhead magazine (founder)

A complete catalog is available on request:

See "Keep in Touch" at back of book for addresses.

LIFE COMES FROM LIFE

Morning walks with His Divine Grace

A. C. Bhaktivedanta Swami Prabhupāda

FOUNDER-ĀCĀRYA OF THE INTERNATIONAL SOCIETY FOR KRISHNA CONSCIOUSNESS

THE BHAKTIVEDANTA BOOK TRUST

Los Angeles • London • Paris • Bombay • Sydney

Readers interested in the subject matter of this book are invited to correspond with the Secretary (for a full list of temples in each country please see the back of this book):

International Society for Krishna Consciousness
P.O. Box 56003, Chatsworth, 4030
S. Africa

International Society for Krishna Consciousness
3764 Watseka Ave. Los Angeles
CA 90034, U.S.A.

International Society for Krishna Consciousness
P.O. Box 262 Botany,
NSW 2019 Australia

International Society for Krishna Consciousness
P.O. Box 324, Borehamwood, Herts.
WD6 1NB, U.K.

Previous Printings: 955,000 copies
Current Printing, 2007: 20,000 copies

Printed in Australia

Library of Congress Catalog Number: 77-95065
ISBN 0-89213-100-4

Contents

Foreword

For people who have come to accept every pronouncement of modern scientists as tested and proven truth, this book will be an eye-opener. *Life Comes From Life* is an impromptu but brilliant critique of some of the dominant policies, theories and presuppositions of modern science and scientists by one of the greatest philosophers and scholars of the century, His Divine Grace A. C. Bhaktivedanta Swami Prabhupāda. Śrīla Prabhupāda's vivid analysis uncovers the hidden and blatantly unfounded assumptions that underlie currently fashionable doctrines concerning the origins and purpose of life.

This book is based on taped morning-walk conversations that Śrīla Prabhupāda had with some of his disciples during 1973, in the Los Angeles area. On those mornings when he focused on science, Śrīla Prabhupāda spoke mainly with his disciple Thoudam D. Singh, Ph.D. An organic chemist, Dr. Singh presently directs the Bhaktivedanta Institute, an international center for advanced study and research in science, philosophy and theology.

Each day, wherever in the world he happened to be, Śrīla Prabhupāda would go out for a lengthy stroll in the chill quietude of the early morning, and cloaked in a warm wrap, he would share intimate moments with a small group of students, disciples and special guests. Some mornings found him immersed in contemplation or quiet appreciation of the surroundings, and little dialogue emerged. At other times he spoke at great length, and often with considerable intensity, on various subjects. During these animated discourses he demonstrated that philosophical analysis need not be a dull, abstruse affair, but can be a dynamic cutting edge into every sphere of life. Nothing could escape his keen intellect, deep spiritual insight and uncommon wit. Rejecting superficial and dogmatic thinking, he edified, challenged, cajoled, charmed and enlightened his students, and he carefully guided them to increased insight and understanding.

Śrīla Prabhupāda (1896–1977) is an internationally recognized author, scholar and spiritual preceptor, and he is widely esteemed as India's greatest cultural ambassador to the world. In *Life Comes*

From Life, Śrīla Prabhupāda takes the role of philosopher–social critic. With philosophical rigor, profound common sense and disarming frankness, he exposes not only modern science's methodological shortcomings and unexamined biases but also the unverified (and unverifiable) speculations that scientists present to the trusting public as known fact. Thus Śrīla Prabhupāda breaks the spell of the materialistic and nihilistic myths which, masquerading as science, have so bewitched modern civilization.

—The Publishers

Introduction

Science: Truth and Fiction

> *"How do you know that the incessant progress of science will not compel scientists . . . to consider that life has existed during eternity, and not matter? . . . How do you know that in 10,000 years one will not consider it more likely that matter has emerged from life?*
>
> —Louis Pasteur

Once upon a time (as in a fairy tale), most of us believed that the food we ate was basically wholesome, nutritious, and free from dangerous chemicals, that advertising was believable, and that product labels truly described the qualities and contents of what we ate. Once upon a time, most of the world believed in the integrity of our heads of state, high-ranking political officials, and local leaders. Once upon a time, we thought our children were getting a solid education in the public schools. Once upon a time, many of us believed atomic energy had "peacetime uses" that were perfectly safe and congruous with a happy and healthy society.

Yet in recent times our illusions have been shattered. Repeated exposés of widespread consumer fraud, grand political scandals, and toxic-waste dumps have all but destroyed our former innocence. We now know that a veil of fantasy and deception can be created with unprecedented expertise through the mass media, making it impossible to distinguish between substance and simulation, reality and illusion.

Scientists as a class have long sat protected in their ivory chambers, exempt from dishonesty. Science, among all other fields, has been regarded as the ultimate meeting ground for seekers and dispensers of truth. The dazzling technological achievements of modern science have given it an aura of infallibility. In *Passages About Earth,* William Irwin Thompson writes, "Just as once there was no appeal from the power of religion without risking damnation, so now there is no appeal from the power of science without risking a charge of irrationality or insanity." But scientists in key academic, industrial, and government positions have shown that they are indeed capable of mixing personal beliefs and ambitions with their research, thus altering the results.

When this happens we are no longer dealing with a search for truth but with a pseudoscience and its resultant array of distortions, fabrications, and false information. Unfortunately, this unscientific method has been applied to the most fundamental field of scientific inquiry—the nature and origin of life. Yet when scientists present untested, unprovable speculations about life's origin, people tend to accept them with blind faith.

Some scientists popularize the notion that a human being is merely a conglomeration of unconscious molecules. But they cannot explain how mere molecules can experience joy upon seeing loved ones, or feel disturbed by the death of one.

A recent exhibit at the Los Angeles Museum of Natural History displayed a number of flasks and beakers. Each contained one of the chemicals found in the human body. The caption explained that although these chemicals represented all the contents of a human body in correct weight and proportion, they could not be considered life, nor could any amount of scientific manipulation bring them to life.

As Michael Polianyi, author of *Atomic Reactions,* notes,

> Current biology is based on the assumption that you can explain the process of life in terms of chemistry and physics; and, of course, physics and chemistry are represented ultimately in terms of forces acting between atomic particles. . . . This is the cause of our corruption of the conception of man, reducing him either to

> an insentient automaton or to a bundle of appetites. This is why science can be invoked so easily in support of totalitarian violence; why science has become the greatest source of dangerous fallacies.

Today many scientists are propagating the doctrine that life originates from matter. Popular works and textbooks posit that life gradually arose from chemicals, a "primordial soup" consisting of amino acids, proteins, and other essential ingredients. However, science cannot provide proof of this, either experimentally or theoretically. In fact these scientists hold their stance essentially on faith even in the face of all sorts of scientific objections. Physicist Hubert Yockey has demonstrated by information theory that even a single informational molecule such as cytochome (what to speak of complex organisms) could not have arisen by chance in the estimated lifetime of the earth: "One must conclude that, contrary to the established and current wisdom, a scenario describing the genesis of life on earth by chance and natural causes which can be accepted on the basis of fact and not faith has not yet been written."

Likewise, some scientists promote the widely-held belief that the sun, stars, planets, galaxies, and conscious life suddenly sprang from a "big bang." Dr. Edwin Godwin, a Princeton University biologist, has compared the chances of a planet such as ours arising from a "big bang" to the likelihood of an unabridged dictionary resulting from an explosion in a printing shop.

The noted biologist W. H. Thorpe writes, "We may be faced with a possibility that the origin of life, like the origin of the universe, becomes an impenetrable barrier to science and a block which resists all attempts to reduce biology to chemistry and physics." And Einstein notes, "Everyone who is seriously involved in the pursuit of science becomes convinced that a spirit is manifest in the laws of the universe—a spirit vastly superior to that of man, and one in the face of which we, with our modest powers, must feel humbled."

Life Comes From Life demonstrates with simple logic that life cannot be reduced to atoms and molecules, and that matter—

without the living force, or spirit—is incapable of generating life in any form. It is also hoped that this book will urge scientists to rededicate themselves to a more genuine and intense quest for truth and knowledge and to thereby redirect their valuable intelligence, resources, and work toward the true benefit of the world.

—Thoudam Damodara Singh, Ph.D.

The First Morning Walk

Recorded on April 18, 1973,
in Cheviot Hills Park, Los Angeles.

Śrīla Prabhupāda is accompanied by Dr. Thoudam Dāmodara Singh, Karandhara dāsa adhikārī, Brahmānanda Svāmī and other students.

Life on Other Planets

ŚRĪLA PRABHUPĀDA. Even on the sun and moon there are living entities. What is the opinion of the scientists?

DR. SINGH. They say there is no life there.

ŚRĪLA PRABHUPĀDA. That is nonsense. There *is* life there.

DR. SINGH. They say that there is no life on the moon because they did not find any there.

ŚRĪLA PRABHUPĀDA. Why do they believe *that*? The moon planet is covered with dust, but within that dust the living entities can live. Every atmosphere is suitable for life—*any* atmosphere. Therefore the *Vedas*[1] describe the living entities as *sarva-gataḥ,* which means "existing in all circumstances." The living entity is not material. Although encaged in a material body, he is not material. But when we speak of different atmospheres, we refer to different material conditions.

KARANDHARA. They say that the moon's atmosphere is unsuitable for life, but all they can legitimately say is that it is unsuitable for life as they know it.

ŚRĪLA PRABHUPĀDA. The *Vedas* say that the living entity has no connection with material things. He cannot be burned, cut, dried up or moistened. This is discussed in *Bhagavad-gītā*.[2]

DR. SINGH. Scientists extend their knowledge about life on this planet, thinking that it must apply to life on other planets also.

ŚRĪLA PRABHUPĀDA. Yes. They are thinking foremost of their own selves. They are thinking limitedly, in terms of their own circumstances. This is what we call "Dr. Frog's philosophy." [Laughter.]

Once there was a frog in a well, and when a friend informed him of the existence of the Atlantic Ocean, he asked the friend, "Oh, what is this Atlantic Ocean?"

"It is a vast body of water," his friend replied.

"How vast? Is it twice the size of this well?"

"Oh, no—much, much larger," his friend replied.

"How much larger? Ten times the size?" In this way, the frog went on calculating. But what is the possibility of ever understanding the vastness of the great ocean in this way? Our faculties, our experience, and our powers of speculation are always limited. The speculations of the scientists only give rise to such frog philosophy.

KARANDHARA. The basis of what they call "scientific integrity" is that they talk only about what they can directly experience.

ŚRĪLA PRABHUPĀDA. You may talk about *your* experience, and I may talk about *my* experience. But why should I accept your experience? You may be a fool, so why should I also become a fool? You may be a frog, but suppose I am a whale. Why should I take your well as all in all? You have your method of acquiring scientific knowledge, and I have mine.

DR. SINGH. Because the scientists haven't detected any water on the surface of the moon, they've concluded that no life could survive there.

ŚRĪLA PRABHUPĀDA. They haven't seen the whole surface of the moon. Suppose someone were to come here from another planet, drop into the Arabian Desert and then return home. Could he come to a complete conclusion about the nature of the whole earth? His knowledge would not be complete.

KARANDHARA. They have a device that senses water. They say they've had it orbit the moon, and they've concluded that the moon has no water and therefore no life.

ŚRĪLA PRABHUPĀDA. Even if, as on the sun, there is apparently no water, still there are living entities there. How does a cactus grow in the desert, apparently without water?

KARANDHARA. It gets water from the atmosphere.

ŚRĪLA PRABHUPĀDA. Yes, because the atmosphere contains all the elements needed to sustain life: earth, water, fire, air and ether. In *anything* material, all these elements are present. For example, in my body there is water, although you cannot see it. Similarly, you don't see fire in my body, yet my body is warm. Where does this warmth come from? You don't see any fire. Do you see any fire burning in my body? Then where does the warmth come from? What is the answer?

The Universe in the Atom

ŚRĪLA PRABHUPĀDA. All matter is a combination of five gross elements (earth, water, fire, air and ether) and three subtle elements (mind, intelligence and false ego).

KARANDHARA. According to the Vedic science, material energy begins with the false ego and then develops into the intelligence, then the mind and then the gross elements—ether, air, fire and so on. So the same basic ingredients are present in all matter. Is this right?

ŚRĪLA PRABHUPĀDA. Yes. The creation of the material universe is like the growth of a great banyan tree[3] from a tiny seed. No one can see the tree within the seed, but all the necessary ingredients for the tree are there, including the required intelligence. Actually, everyone's body is simply a sample universe. Your body and my body are different universes, small universes. Therefore, all eight material elements are present within our bodies, just as they are within the whole universe. Similarly, an insect's body is another universe.

KARANDHARA. How about the atom?

ŚRĪLA PRABHUPĀDA. The same formula applies: all these constituents are within the atom. *Aṇor aṇīyān mahato mahīyān* [*Kaṭha Upaniṣad* 1.2.20]. This means that whether something is extremely large or infinitesimal, it is still made of the same basic elements. This is true everywhere in the material world. Just as a woman's small watch has all the requisite machinery for its smooth functioning, so an ant has all the necessary brain substance to manage its affairs nicely. How is this possible? To answer this properly, you must minutely examine the brain tissues in the ant. But this you cannot do. Moreover, there are *innumerable* insects smaller than the ant. So there must be a mechanical arrangement for all this detailed activity, but scientists cannot discover it.

Relativity and Knowledge

ŚRĪLA PRABHUPĀDA. All living entities possess the required intelligence to execute four principles: eating, sleeping, sexual intercourse and defense. These four principles exist even in the atom. The only difference in the human being is that he has the extra intelligence with which to understand God. This is the difference. *Āhāra-nidrā-bhaya-maithunaṁ ca sāmānam etat paśubhir narāṇām.* Eating, sleeping, sex life and defense are to be found everywhere. You have seen trees growing. Wherever there is a knot, the bark does not go *this* way; it goes *that* way. [Śrīla Prabhupāda gestures to show that a tree's bark grows not over a knot, but around it.] The tree has intelligence: "If I go this way, I will be blocked, so I will go that way." But where are its eyes? How can it see? It has *intelligence.* That intelligence may not be as good as yours, but it *is* intelligence. Similarly, a child also has intelligence, though not as developed as his father's. In due course of time, when the child gets a body like that of his father, the child's intelligence will be fully developed and exhibited.

DR. SINGH. Then intelligence is relative.

ŚRĪLA PRABHUPĀDA. Yes. Everything is relative. You have your body, your duration of life, and your intelligence, and the ant has his. Both we and the ant live for one hundred years, but the length of our hundred-year life-span is relative to our bodies. Even Brahmā, the longest-living entity in this universe, lives for one hundred years. To us the ant's life-span may seem only a few days. In the same way, on other planets with atmospheres different from the earth's, there are life-forms suited to those conditions. But the scientists try to view everything according to the relative conditions of planet earth. This is nonsense. Why are they doing that? If the whole cosmic manifestation follows the law of relativity, how can the scientist say that the conditions of this planet must apply to life on other planets?

The *Vedas* instruct us that knowledge must always be considered in terms of *deśa-kāla-pātra. Deśa* means "circumstances," *kāla* means "time," and *pātra* means "the object." We must understand everything by taking these three elements into consideration. For example, a fish is living very comfortably in the water, and we are shivering on the shore of the sea. This is because my *deśa-kāla-pātra* and the fish's *deśa-kāla-pātra* are different. But if we conclude that the sea gulls will also shiver in the water, that is nonsense; their *deśa-kāla-pātra* is again different. There are 8,400,000 different species of life in the material cosmic manifestation, and each species must adjust to circumstances differently. Even on this planet, you cannot go live comfortably in Alaska, although it is America. Similarly, the living entities enjoying life in Alaska do not come here.

KARANDHARA. Relativity, then, is based upon our individual situation.

ŚRĪLA PRABHUPĀDA. Yes. Therefore it is said that what is food for one is poison for another.

BRAHMĀNANDA SVĀMĪ. Because scientists cannot survive on the moon, they think no one else can.

The 8.6-Billion-Year Day

DR. SINGH. The problem with the world is that practically everyone is thinking only in terms of his own circumstances—and that is nonsense.

STUDENT. Someone who has never gone out of his village thinks that his village is the whole world.

ŚRĪLA PRABHUPĀDA. Yes. The frog is always thinking in terms relative to his well. He has no power to think otherwise. The ocean is great, but he is thinking of the ocean's greatness in terms relative to his *own* greatness. Similarly, God is great, but we are thinking of God in terms of relative greatness, greatness relative to our own. There are certain insects that are born at night, and they grow, bear offspring and die—all before daybreak. They never see the morning. So if they conclude that there is no morning, that is nonsense. In the same way, as soon as we hear from the *śāstras* [revealed scriptures] that Brahmā's duration of life is equivalent to millions of our years, we do not believe it. We say, "How can it be?" But *Bhagavad-gītā* [8.17] says, *sahasra-yuga-paryantam ahar yad brahmaṇo viduḥ:* "Four billion three hundred million earth years equal Brahmā's twelve hours." Even a leading Indian politician who was known as a great scholar of the *Gītā* could not accept this information. He said it is mental speculation. Such a rascal! Yet he is passing as an important scholar. This is the problem. Rascals and fools are passing as scholars, scientists and philosophers, and therefore the whole world is being misguided.

The Second Morning Walk

Recorded on April 19, 1973,
in Cheviot Hills Park, Los Angeles.

Śrīla Prabhupāda is accompanied by Dr. Singh, Karandhara dāsa adhikārī, Brahmānanda Svāmī and other students.

Darwinism Extinct

ŚRĪLA PRABHUPĀDA. This material world is a composition of three qualities—*sattva, rajas* and *tamas* (goodness, passion and ignorance)—which are working everywhere. These three qualities are present in various proportions in all species of life. For example, some trees produce nice fruit, while others are simply meant for fuel. This is due to the association of particular qualities of nature. Among animals also, these three qualities are present. The cow is in the quality of goodness, the lion in passion, and the monkey in ignorance. According to Darwin, Darwin's father is a monkey. [Laughter.] He has theorized foolishly.

DR. SINGH. Darwin has said that some species become extinct in the struggle for survival. Those which are capable of surviving will survive, but those which are not will become extinct. So he says survival and extinction go side by side.

ŚRĪLA PRABHUPĀDA. Nothing is extinct. The monkey is not extinct. Darwin's immediate forefather, the monkey, is still existing.

KARANDHARA. Darwin said there must be a natural selection. But selection means choice. So who is choosing?

ŚRĪLA PRABHUPĀDA. That must be a person. Who is allowing someone to survive and someone to be killed? There must be some authority with discretion to give such an order. That is our first proposition. Who that authority is, is explained in

Bhagavad-gītā. Kṛṣṇa says, *mayādhyakṣeṇa prakṛtiḥ:* "Nature is working under My supervision." [Bg. 9.10]

DR. SINGH. Darwin also says that the different species were not created simultaneously, but evolved gradually.

ŚRĪLA PRABHUPĀDA. Then what is his explanation for how the process of evolution began?

KARANDHARA. Modern proponents of Darwinism say that the first living organism was created chemically.

ŚRĪLA PRABHUPĀDA. And I say to them, "If life originated from chemicals, and if your science is so advanced, then why can't *you* create life biochemically in your laboratories?"

In the Future

KARANDHARA. They say they will create life in the future.

ŚRĪLA PRABHUPĀDA. What future? When this crucial point is raised, they reply, "We shall do it in the future." Why in the future? That is nonsense. "Trust no future, however pleasant." If they are so advanced, they must demonstrate *now* how life can be created from chemicals. Otherwise what is the meaning of their advancement? They are talking nonsense.

KARANDHARA. They say that they are right on the verge of creating life.

ŚRĪLA PRABHUPĀDA. That's only a different way of saying the same thing: "In the future." The scientists must admit that they still do not know the origin of life. Their claim that they will soon prove a chemical origin of life is something like paying someone with a postdated check. Suppose I give you a postdated check for ten thousand dollars but I actually have no money. What is the value of that check? Scientists are claiming that their science is wonderful, but when a practical example is wanted, they say they will provide it in the future. Suppose I say that I possess millions of dollars, and when you ask me for some money I say, "Yes, I will now give you a big postdated check. Is that all right?" If you are intelligent, you will reply, "At present give me at least five dollars in cash so I can see something tangible." Similarly, the scientists cannot produce even a single blade of grass in their laboratories, yet they are claiming that life is produced from chemicals. What is this nonsense? Is no one questioning this?

KARANDHARA. They say that life is produced by chemical laws.

ŚRĪLA PRABHUPĀDA. As soon as there is a law, we must take into consideration that someone made the law. Despite all their so-called advancement, the scientists in their laboratories cannot produce even a blade of grass. What kind of scientists are they?

DR. SINGH. They say that in the ultimate analysis, everything came from matter. Living matter came from nonliving matter.

ŚRĪLA PRABHUPĀDA. Then where is this living matter coming from now? Do the scientists say that life came from matter in the past but does not at the present? Where is the ant coming from now—from the dirt?

The Missing Link

DR. SINGH. In fact, there are several theories explaining how life originated from matter, how living matter came from the non-living.

ŚRĪLA PRABHUPĀDA [casting Dr. Singh in the role of a materialistic scientist]. All right, scientist, why is life not coming from matter now? You rascal. Why isn't life coming from matter now?

Actually such scientists are rascals. They childishly say that life came from matter, although they are not at all able to prove it. Our Kṛṣṇa consciousness movement should expose all these rascals. They are only bluffing. Why don't they create life immediately? In the past, they say, life arose from matter; and they say that this will happen again in the future. They even say that they will create life from matter. What kind of theory is this? They have already commented that life began from matter. This refers to the past—"began." Then why do they now speak of the future? Is it not contradictory? They are expecting the past to occur in the future. This is childish nonsense.

KARANDHARA. They say that life arose from matter in the past and that they will create life this way in the future.

ŚRĪLA PRABHUPĀDA. What is this nonsense? If they cannot prove that life arises from matter in the present, how do they know life arose this way in the past?

DR. SINGH. They are assuming . . .

ŚRĪLA PRABHUPĀDA. Everyone can assume, but this is not science. Everyone can assume something. You can assume something, I can assume something. But there must be proof. We can *prove* that life arises from life. For example, a father begets a child. The father is living, and the child is living. But where is their proof that a father can be a dead stone? *Where is their proof?* We can easily prove that life begins from life. And the original life is Kṛṣṇa. That also can be proven. But what evidence exists that a child is born of stone? They cannot actually prove that life comes from matter. They are leaving that aside for the future. [Laughter.]

KARANDHARA. The scientists say that they can now formulate acids, amino acids, that are almost like one-celled living organisms. They say that because these acids so closely resemble living beings, there must be just one missing link needed before they can create life.

ŚRĪLA PRABHUPĀDA. Nonsense! Missing link. I'll challenge them to their face! [Laughter.] They are missing this challenge. The missing link is this challenge to their face.

Nobel Prize for an Ass

DR. SINGH. Some scientists hope that in the future they will be able to make babies in test tubes.

ŚRĪLA PRABHUPĀDA. Test tubes?

DR. SINGH. Yes, they intend to combine male and female elements in biological laboratories.

ŚRĪLA PRABHUPĀDA. If they begin with living entities, what is the purpose of the test tube? It is only a place for combination, but so is the womb. Where is the credit for the scientists if this is already being done in nature's test tube?

KARANDHARA. It is already being done by nature, but when some scientist does it, people will give him the Nobel Prize.

ŚRĪLA PRABHUPĀDA. Yes, that is stated in *Śrīmad-Bhāgavatam: śva-viḍ-varāhoṣṭra-kharaiḥ saṁstutaḥ puruṣaḥ paśuḥ.*[4] This verse indicates that those who praise men who are like animals are no better than dogs, hogs, camels and asses. *Śva* means "dog," *viḍ-*

varāha means "stool-eating hog," *uṣṭra* means "camel," and *khara* means "ass." If the Nobel Prize is given to a scientist who is a rascal, the men on the committee who give him that prize are no better than dogs, hogs, camels and asses. We don't accept them as human beings. One animal is praised by another animal. Where is the credit in that? If the men on the committee are no better than animals, anyone who receives the Nobel Prize in science is fool number one, because animals are praising him, not human beings.

DR. SINGH. For some scientists, the Nobel Prize is the ultimate.

ŚRĪLA PRABHUPĀDA. They are rascals. They are speaking nonsense, and because they are juggling words, others are being misled.

BRAHMĀNANDA SVĀMĪ. Nobel is the person who invented dynamite.

ŚRĪLA PRABHUPĀDA. He has created great misfortune, and he has left his money for creating further misfortune. [Laughter.]

BRAHMĀNANDA SVĀMĪ. The *Gītā* says that demoniac people perform acts meant to destroy the world.

ŚRĪLA PRABHUPĀDA. Yes. *Ugra-karmāṇaḥ kṣayāya jagato 'hitaḥ* [Bg. 16.9]. They perform acts meant for inauspiciousness and the destruction of the world.

The Difference Between the Living and the Nonliving

[Śrīla Prabhupāda points at a dead tree with his cane.]

ŚRĪLA PRABHUPĀDA. Formerly leaves and twigs were growing from this tree. Now they are not. How would the scientists explain this?

KARANDHARA. They would say the tree's chemical composition has changed.

ŚRĪLA PRABHUPĀDA. To prove that theory, they must be able to inject the proper chemicals to make branches and leaves grow again. The scientific method includes observation, hypothesis and then demonstration. Then it is perfect. But the scientists cannot actually demonstrate in their laboratories that life comes from matter. They simply observe and then speak nonsense. They are like children. In our childhood, we observed a gramophone box and thought that within the box was a man singing, an electric man. We thought there must have been an electric man or some kind of ghost in it. [Laughter.]

DR. SINGH. One of the popular questions that arises when we start studying biology is "What is the difference between a living organism and that which is not living?" The textbooks say that the chief characteristics that distinguish the two are that a living being can move and reproduce, whereas dead matter can do neither. But the books never talk about the nature of the soul or about the consciousness of the living entity.

ŚRĪLA PRABHUPĀDA. But consciousness is the primary indication that life is present. Only because of consciousness can a living being move and reproduce. Because a person is conscious, he thinks of marrying, and begetting children. And the original consciousness is described in the *Vedas: tad aikṣata bahu syām* [*Chāndogya Upaniṣad* 6.2.3]. This means that God, the original conscious being, said, "I shall become many." Without consciousness, there is no possibility of by-products.

The Individual Living Force

ŚRĪLA PRABHUPĀDA. The gardeners supply water to the green trees, so why don't they supply water to this dead tree and make it green?

DR. SINGH. From experience they know that it will not grow.

ŚRĪLA PRABHUPĀDA. Then what is the element that is lacking? Scientists say that chemicals are the cause of life, but all the chemicals that were present when the tree was alive are still there. And these chemicals are still supporting the lives of many living entities such as microbes and insects. So they cannot say that life energy is lacking in the body of the tree. The life energy is there.

DR. SINGH. But what about the life energy of the tree itself?

ŚRĪLA PRABHUPĀDA. Yes, that is the difference. The living force is individual, and the particular individual living entity that was the tree has left. This must be the case, since all the chemicals necessary to support life are still there, yet the tree is dead.

Here is another example. Suppose I am living in an apartment, and then I leave it. I am gone, but many other living entities remain there—ants, spiders and so forth. So it is not true that simply because I have left the apartment, it can no longer accommodate life. Other living entities are still living there. It is simply that I—an individual living being—have left. The chemicals in the tree are like the apartment: they are simply the environment for the individual force—the soul—to act through. And the soul is an individual. I am an individual, and therefore I may leave the apartment. Similarly, the microbes are also individuals; they have individual consciousness. If they are moving in one direction but are somehow blocked, they think, "Let me go the other way." They have *personality.*

KARANDHARA. But in a dead body there is no personality.

ŚRĪLA PRABHUPĀDA. This indicates that the individual soul has left that body. The soul has left, and therefore the tree does not grow.

DR. SINGH. Within the living body, Śrīla Prabhupāda, there are innumerable small living entities, but the individual self who owns the body is also living there. Is that correct?

ŚRĪLA PRABHUPĀDA. Yes. In my body there are millions of living entities. In my intestines there are many worms. If they become strong, then whatever I eat, they eat, and I derive no benefit from the food. Therefore those who are full of hookworms eat very much but do not grow. They become lean and thin, and they are very hungry, because these small living entities are eating their food. So there are thousands and millions of living entities in my body—they are individuals, and I am an individual—but I am the proprietor of the body, just as I may be the proprietor of a garden in which many millions of living entities reside.

STUDENT. So if I eat *kṛṣṇa-prasāda* [food offered to Lord Kṛṣṇa], are the living entities in my body also eating *prasāda*?

ŚRĪLA PRABHUPĀDA. Yes. You are very benevolent. [Laughs.] You take *kṛṣṇa-prasāda* for others.

KARANDHARA. Welfare work.

ŚRĪLA PRABHUPĀDA. Yes, but there are so many things within you for them to eat that you do not need to make a separate endeavor to feed them.

Minimum Words, Maximum Solution

ŚRĪLA PRABHUPĀDA. The individual soul is never lost. He does not die, nor is he born. He simply changes from one body to another, just as one changes garments. This is perfect science.

DR. SINGH. But why don't scientists accept this?

ŚRĪLA PRABHUPĀDA. They are not nice men. They are rascals. They are not even gentlemen. Under appropriate circumstances, gentlemen will have some shyness or some shame. But these men are shameless. They cannot properly answer our challenges, yet they shamelessly claim that they are scientists and that they will create life. They are not even gentlemen. At least *I* regard them like that. A gentleman will be ashamed to speak nonsense.

DR. SINGH. They do not think before they speak.

ŚRĪLA PRABHUPĀDA. That means that they are not human beings. A human being thinks twice before saying anything. Kṛṣṇa makes the presence of life within the body so easy to understand. He says:

dehino 'smin yathā dehe
kaumāraṁ yauvanaṁ jarā
tathā dehāntara-prāptir
dhīras tatra na muhyati

["As the embodied soul continually passes, in this body, from boyhood to youth to old age, the soul similarly passes into another body at death. The self-realized soul is not bewildered by such a change." (Bg. 2.13)] In these two lines, Kṛṣṇa solves the whole biological problem. That is knowledge. Minimum words, maximum solution. Volumes of books expounding nonsense have no meaning. Materialistic scientists are like croaking frogs: *ka-ka-ka, ka-ka-ka.* [Śrīla Prabhupāda imitates the sound of a croaking frog, and the others laugh.] The frogs are thinking, "Oh, we are talking very nicely," but the result is that the snake finds them and says, "Oh, here is a nice frog!" [Śrīla Prabhupāda imitates the sound of a snake eating a frog.] *Bup!* Finished. When death comes, everything is finished. The materialistic scientists are croaking—*ka-ka-ka*—but when death comes, their scientific industry is finished, and they become dogs, cats or something like that.

The Third Morning Walk

Recorded on April 28, 1973,
in Cheviot Hills Park, Los Angeles.

Śrīla Prabhupāda is accompanied by Dr. Singh, Karandhara dāsa adhikārī and other students.

Scientists as Thieves

ŚRĪLA PRABHUPĀDA [holding a rose in his hand]. Can any scientist create a flower like this in the laboratory?

DR. SINGH. That is not possible.

ŚRĪLA PRABHUPĀDA. No, it is not. Just see how wonderfully Kṛṣṇa's energy is working! No scientist can create a flower like this in his laboratory. They cannot create even a few grains of sand, yet they claim to possess the most advanced intellects in the universe. This is foolish.

DR. SINGH. They take matter from Kṛṣṇa, manipulate it, and then claim that *they* have created something wonderful.

ŚRĪLA PRABHUPĀDA. At least if they would admit that they have taken the matter from Kṛṣṇa, that would be good. We understand that everything comes from Kṛṣṇa.

DR. SINGH. But they will not admit that they are taking anything from Kṛṣṇa. Instead they say that *they* are the creators.

ŚRĪLA PRABHUPĀDA. How have they created anything? They take the sand and mix it with some chemicals and make glass. They have not created the sand or the chemicals; they have taken them from the earth. How have they created anything?

DR. SINGH. They say, "We have taken the materials from nature."

ŚRĪLA PRABHUPĀDA. "From nature" means from a person. They have taken from nature, but they are thieves because everything in nature belongs to Kṛṣṇa. *Īśāvāsyam idaṁ sarvam:* "Everything is God's creation." [*Īśopaniṣad* 1] In *Bhagavad-gītā*

Kṛṣṇa states that if one does not perform *yajña* [sacrifice], he is a thief. *Yajña* means acknowledging that things have been taken from Kṛṣṇa. We should think, "Kṛṣṇa, You have given us many, many things for our maintenance." *This* much acknowledgment Kṛṣṇa wants; that's all. Otherwise, what can He expect from *you*? What are you in His presence? We should acknowledge Kṛṣṇa's kindness. Therefore, before we eat we offer the food to Kṛṣṇa and say, "Kṛṣṇa, You have given us this nice food, so first You taste it." Then we eat it.

Kṛṣṇa is not hungry, yet He can eat the whole world and then again produce it exactly as it was. *Pūrṇasya pūrṇam ādāya pūrṇam evāvaśiṣyate* [*Īśopaniṣad* Invocation]. Kṛṣṇa is so perfect that if you take from Kṛṣṇa all of Kṛṣṇa's energy, all the original energy is still with Him. *That* is perfect conservation of energy.

The Origin of Nature

DR. SINGH. There is a scientific journal called *Nature*. It contains articles concerning natural products like plants, flowers and minerals, but it does not mention God.

ŚRĪLA PRABHUPĀDA. We may rightly observe that plants are being produced by nature. But the next question we must ask is, "Who has produced nature?" To ask *this* is real intelligence.

DR. SINGH. They don't generally think about this.

ŚRĪLA PRABHUPĀDA. Then they are foolish. Where does nature come from? As soon as we speak of nature, the next question should be, "*Whose* nature?" Is it not so? For instance, I speak of *my* nature, and you speak of *your* nature. Therefore, as soon as we speak of nature, the next inquiry should be, "*Whose* nature?" Nature means energy. And as soon as we speak of energy, we must inquire into the source of that energy. For example, if you speak of electric energy, you must accept its source, the powerhouse. How can you deny it? Electricity does not come to us automatically. Similarly, nature is not working automatically; it is under the control of Kṛṣṇa.

STUDENT. In the *Vedas* it is said that material energy works under Kṛṣṇa's direction.

ŚRĪLA PRABHUPĀDA. Yes. As soon as you speak of energy, there must be a source.

The Mirage of the Material World

KARANDHARA. Geologists study the strata of the earth's crust to trace out the origin of the earth.

ŚRĪLA PRABHUPĀDA. But these strata are being created and destroyed at every moment. Now they are one way, and a half hour from now they will be different. They are *jagat,* always changing. Kṛṣṇa states in *Bhagavad-gītā* [8.4], *adhibhūtaṁ kṣaro bhāvaḥ:* "Physical nature is known to be endlessly mutable." Therefore, one cannot find out the source of all energy simply by observing the energy itself. Now the earth's strata may be black, later they may be white, and then again black. So the geologists study the black color, then the white color, again the black, and so on. This is called *punaḥ punaś carvita-carvaṇānām,* "chewing the chewed."[5] Now it is cold, at midday it will be warm, and at night it will be cold again. In this way, the entire material cosmic manifestation is subject to different types of change. Even our bodies are changing. Everything is changing. But what is the eternity behind this changing? That is the subject of real knowledge. The scientists do not find that eternity, and therefore they are disappointed. They think that the background of everything is void, zero. They think that eternity is zero. And when they are asked where this zero comes from, they say, "It comes from nothing." So we must ask them, "How have the varieties come about?" The Vedic conclusion is that variety is eternal, although the changing varieties the scientists study in the material world are temporary. These varieties are shadow varieties. Real variety exists eternally in the spiritual world.

DR. SINGH. So the material universe is like a mirage?

ŚRĪLA PRABHUPĀDA. Yes. Suppose I think I see water in the desert when there is not water. This is an illusion. Water exists, but not in the mirage. Similarly, the material varieties we see—the varieties of enjoyment—are like that mirage. We, the living entities, are meant for enjoyment, but we are seeking enjoyment in a false place—in an illusion. We are like the desert animals who run after water in a mirage and eventually die of thirst. They cannot relieve their thirst with such illusory water. Similarly, we are trying to manufacture many things to satisfy our thirst for enjoyment, but we are being baffled at every turn because material existence is an illusion. Therefore real intelligence means to inquire, "Where is the reality? Where is the eternal substance behind the illusion?" If we can find *that* out, we can experience real enjoyment.

The Fourth Morning Walk

Recorded on April, 29, 1973,
on the shores of the Pacific Ocean near Los Angeles.

Śrīla Prabhupāda is accompanied by Dr. Singh, Brahmānanda Svāmī, Karandhara dāsa adhikārī and other students.

The Progress of the Asses

Śrīla Prabhupāda. Everyone is suffering here in the material world, and scientific improvement means that the scientists are creating a situation of further suffering. That's all. They are not making improvements. Bhaktivinoda Ṭhākura[6] confirms this by saying, *moha janamiyā, anitya saṁsāre, jīvake karaye gādhā:* "By so-called scientific improvements, the scientist has become an ass." Moreover, he is becoming a better and better ass, and nothing more. Suppose that by working very hard like an ass, a person builds a skyscraper. He may engage in a lifelong labor for this, but ultimately he must die. He cannot stay; he will be kicked out of his skyscraper, because material life is impermanent. Scientists are constantly doing research, and if you ask them what they are doing, they say, "Oh, it is for the next generation, for the future." But I say, "What about *you*? What about your skyscraper? If in your next life you are going to be a tree, what will you do with your next generation then?" But he is an ass. He does not know that he is going to stand before his skyscraper for ten thousand years. And what about the next generation? If there is no petrol, what will the next generation do? And how will the next generation help him if he is going to be a cat, a dog or a tree?

The scientists—and everyone else—should endeavor to achieve freedom from the repetition of birth and death. But instead, everyone is becoming more and more entangled in the cycle of birth and death. *Bhave 'smin kliśyamānānām avidyā-kāma-karmabhiḥ.* This is a quotation from *Śrīmad-Bhāgavatam* [1.8.35]. Here in one line the whole material existence is explained. *This* is literature. This one line is worth thousands of years of research work. It explains how the living entity is taking birth in this world, where he comes from, where he is going, what his activities should be, and many other essential things. The words *bhave 'smin kliśyamānānām* refer to the struggle for existence. Why does this struggle exist? Because of *avidyā,* ignorance. And what is the nature of that ignorance? *Kāma-karmabhiḥ,* being forced to work simply for the senses, or in other words, entanglement in material sense gratification.

STUDENT. So, is it true that modern scientific research increases the demands of the body because the scientist is ultimately working to gratify his senses?

ŚRĪLA PRABHUPĀDA. Yes.

Word Jugglery and World Crisis

ŚRĪLA PRABHUPĀDA. It is said in the *Vedas, yasmin vijñāte sarvam evaṁ vijñātaṁ bhavati:* "If one knows the Absolute Truth, then all other things become known." I am not a Ph.D., yet I can challenge the scientists. Why? Because I know Kṛṣṇa, the Absolute Truth. *Yasmin sthito na duḥkhena guruṇāpi vicālyate:* "If one is situated in Kṛṣṇa consciousness, then even in the greatest calamities he will not be disturbed." [Bg. 6.22] *Śrīmad-Bhāgavatam* [1.5.22] declares, *avicyuto 'rthaḥ kavibhir nirūpito yad uttamaśloka-guṇānuvarṇanam:* "Great personalities have decided that Kṛṣṇa consciousness is the perfection of life." This kind of knowledge is required. Not that we do some research, come up with a theory, and after fifteen years say, "No, no, it is not right—it is another thing." That is not science; that is child's play.

DR. SINGH. That is how they discover things—by research.

ŚRĪLA PRABHUPĀDA. And what is the *cost* of the research? It is a scientific method for drawing money from others, that's all. In other words, it is cheating. Scientists juggle words like *plutonium, photons, hydrogen* and *oxygen,* but what good will people get from this? When people hear this jugglery of words, what can they say? One scientist explains something to some extent, and then another rascal comes along and explains it again, but differently, with different words. And all the time the phenomenon has remained the same. What advancement has been made? They have simply produced volumes of books. Now there is a petrol problem. Scientists have created it. If the petrol supply dwindles away, what will these rascal scientists do? They are powerless to do anything about it.

The Billion-Dollar Dustheap

ŚRĪLA PRABHUPĀDA. Now there is a scarcity of water in India, but what are the scientists doing about it? There is more than enough water in the world, so why don't the scientists bring water where it is urgently required? They should employ irrigation immediately. But instead they are going to the moon, the dusty planet, to make it fertile. Why don't they irrigate *this* planet? There's plenty of seawater, so why don't they irrigate the Sahara or the Arabian or Rajasthani Desert? "Yes," they say, "in the future. We are trying." In their pride, they immediately say, "Yes, yes. We are trying." In *Bhagavad-gītā* it is said that when one is engaged in the business of satisfying unnecessary desires, he becomes bereft of all intelligence (*kāmais tais tair hṛta-jñānāḥ*).

This moon project is childish. Those who aspire to go to the moon are like crying children. A child cries, "Mother, give me the moon," so the mother gives the child a mirror and says, "Here is the moon, my dear son." And the child takes the mirror, sees the moon in it and says, "Oh, I have the moon." Unfortunately, this is not just a story.

KARANDHARA. After spending all that money to go to the moon and bring back just a few rocks, the people on the space project decided that there was nothing more to do there.

BRAHMĀNANDA SVĀMĪ. Now they want to go to another planet, but they are short of money. Going to other planets costs millions and billions of dollars.

ŚRĪLA PRABHUPĀDA. People work very hard while the rascal government takes taxes and spends money unnecessarily. There should be no sympathy when so much hard-earned money comes from the public and is spent so foolishly. Now the leaders are presenting another bluff: "Don't worry, we are going to another planet. Now we shall bring *more* dust. We shall bring tons of dust. Oh, yes, now we shall have tons of dust."

DR. SINGH. They believe there may be life on Mars.

ŚRĪLA PRABHUPĀDA. They may believe or not believe. What is the difference? Life exists *here,* but people are fighting. So suppose there is life on Mars. There *is* life on Mars, undoubtedly. But what will we gain from this?

DR. SINGH. People are curious to know what is going on there.

ŚRĪLA PRABHUPĀDA. That means that for their childish curiosity they must spend vast sums of money. Just see the fun. And when they are asked to help one of the many poverty-stricken countries, they say, "No. No money." Do you see?

Sāṅkhya Philosophy and Modern Science

DR. SINGH. Śrīla Prabhupāda, may we hear a little bit about Sāṅkhya philosophy?

ŚRĪLA PRABHUPĀDA. There are actually two kinds of Sāṅkhya philosophy: the ancient Sāṅkhya philosophy originally taught by Lord Kapiladeva, and the modern Sāṅkhya philosophy taught more recently by the atheist Kapila. Lord Kapila's Sāṅkhya explains how to become detached from matter and search out Lord Viṣṇu within the heart. This Sāṅkhya is actually a process of devotional service. But the modern Sāṅkhya philosophy simply analyzes the material world into its various elements. In that respect, it is just like modern scientific research. *Sāṅkhya* means "to count." We are also Sāṅkhya philosophers to some extent because we count the material elements: this is land, this is water, this is fire, this is air, this is ether. Furthermore, I can count my mind, my intelligence and my ego. Beyond my ego, however, I cannot count. But Kṛṣṇa says that there *is* something beyond the ego, and that is the living force. This is what scientists do not know. They think that life is merely a combination of material elements, but Kṛṣṇa denies this in the *Bhagavad-gītā* [7.5]:

apareyam itas tv anyāṁ
prakṛtiṁ viddhi me parām

jīva-bhūtāṁ mahā-bāho
yayedaṁ dhāryate jagat

"Besides this inferior nature [earth, water, fire, air, ether, mind, intelligence and false ego] there is a superior energy of Mine, which consists of all the living entities who are struggling with material nature and sustaining the universe."

DR. SINGH. Are both the inferior and the superior energies studied in modern Sāṅkhya philosophy?

ŚRĪLA PRABHUPĀDA. No. Modern Sāṅkhya philosophers do not study the superior energy. They simply analyze the material elements, just as the scientists are doing. The scientists do not know that there is spirit soul, nor do the Sāṅkhya philosophers.

DR. SINGH. They are analyzing the creative material elements?

ŚRĪLA PRABHUPĀDA. The material elements are not creative! Only the soul is creative. Life cannot be created from matter, and matter cannot create itself. You, a living entity, can mix hydrogen and oxygen to create water. But matter itself has no creative potency. If you place a bottle of hydrogen near a bottle of oxygen, will they automatically combine, without your help?

DR. SINGH. No. They must be mixed.

ŚRĪLA PRABHUPĀDA. Of course. Oxygen and hydrogen are Kṛṣṇa's inferior energy, but when you, the superior energy, mix them, then they can become water.

The Remote Cause and the Immediate Cause

ŚRĪLA PRABHUPĀDA. Inferior energy has no power unless superior energy is involved. This sea [indicating the Pacific Ocean] is calm and quiet. But when the superior force, air, pushes it, it manifests high waves. The ocean has no power to move without the superior force of the air. Similarly, there is another force superior to the air, and another and another, until ultimately we arrive at Kṛṣṇa. This is real research.

Kṛṣṇa controls nature just as an engineer controls a train. The engineer controls the locomotive, which pulls one car, and that car in turn pulls another, which pulls another, and so the whole train is moving. Similarly, with the creation, Kṛṣṇa gives the first push, and then, by means of successive pushes, the entire cosmic manifestation comes into being and is maintained. This is explained in *Bhagavad-gītā* [9.10]. *Mayādhyakṣeṇa prakṛtiḥ sūyate sacarācaram:* "This material nature is working under My direction and is producing all moving and unmoving beings." And in the Fourteenth Chapter [14.4] Kṛṣṇa says:

sarva-yoniṣu kaunteya
mūrtayaḥ sambhavanti yāḥ
tāsāṁ brahma mahad yonir
ahaṁ bīja-pradaḥ pitā

"All species of life are made possible by birth in this material nature, O son of Kuntī, and I am the seed-giving father." For example, if we sow a banyan seed, a huge tree eventually comes up and, along with it, millions of new seeds. Each of these seeds can in turn produce another tree with millions of new seeds, and so on. This is how Kṛṣṇa, the original seed-giving father, is the primary cause of everything we see.

Unfortunately, the scientists observe only the immediate cause; they cannot perceive the remote cause. Kṛṣṇa is described in the *Vedas* as *sarva-kāraṇa-kāraṇam,* the cause of all causes. If one understands the cause of all causes, then he understands everything. *Yasmin vijñāte sarvam evaṁ vijñātaṁ bhavati:* "If one knows the original cause, the subordinate causes are automatically known." Although the scientists are searching after the original cause, when the *Vedas,* perfect knowledge, declare the original cause to be the Supreme Personality of Godhead, the scientists won't accept it. They keep to their partial, imperfect knowledge. This is their disease.

The Cosmic Machine

ŚRĪLA PRABHUPĀDA. Scientists do not know that there are two types of energy—inferior and superior—although they are actually working with these two energies every day. Material energy can never work independently; it must first come in contact with spiritual energy. So how can people accept that the entire cosmic manifestation, which is nothing but matter, has come about automatically? A competent machine does not work unless a man who knows how to work it pushes a button. A Cadillac is a nice car, but if it has no driver, what is the use of it? So the material universe is also a machine.

People are amazed at seeing a big machine with many, many parts, but an intelligent person knows that however wonderful a machine may be, it does not work unless an operator comes and pushes the proper button. Therefore, who is more important—the operator or the machine? So we are concerned not with the material machine—this cosmic manifestation—but with its operator, Kṛṣṇa. Now you may say, "Well, how do I *know* that He is the operator?" Kṛṣṇa says, *mayādhyakṣeṇa prakṛtiḥ sūyate sacarācaram:* "Under My direction the whole cosmic manifestation is working." If you say, "No, Kṛṣṇa is not the operator behind the cosmos," then you have to accept another operator, and you must *present* him. But this you cannot do. Therefore, in the absence of your proof, you should accept mine.

The Fifth Morning Walk

Recorded on May 3, 1973,
on the shores of the Pacific Ocean near Los Angeles.

Śrīla Prabhupāda is accompanied by Dr. Singh and Brahmānanda Svāmī.

The Invisible Pilot

ŚRĪLA PRABHUPĀDA. Almost everyone in the world is under the false impression that life is born from matter. We cannot allow this nonsensical theory to go unchallenged. Life does not come from matter. Matter is generated from life. This is not theory; it is fact. Science is based on an incorrect theory; therefore all its calculations and conclusions are wrong, and people are suffering because of this. When all these mistaken modern scientific theories are corrected, people will become happy. So we must challenge the scientists and defeat them; otherwise they will mislead the entire society. Matter changes in six phases: birth, growth, maintenance, production of by-products, dwindling and death. But the life within matter, the spirit soul, is eternal; it goes through no such changes. Life *appears* to be developing and decaying, but actually it is simply passing through each of these six phases until the material body can no longer be maintained. Then the old body dies, and the soul enters a new body. When our clothing is old and worn, we change it. Similarly, one day our bodies become old and useless, and we pass on to a new body.

As Kṛṣṇa says in the *Bhagavad-gītā* [2.13], *dehino 'smin yathā dehe kaumāraṁ yauvanaṁ jarā/ tathā dehāntara-prāptiḥ:* "As the embodied soul continually passes, in this body, from boyhood to youth to old age, the soul similarly passes into another body at death." And a little later [2.18]: *antavanta ime dehā nityasyoktāḥ śarīriṇaḥ.* This means that only the material body of the indestructible and eternal living entity is subject to destruction. The material body is perishable, but the life within the body is *nitya,* eternal.

Everything works on the basis of this living force. This is the Pacific Ocean, and these high waves are being manipulated by living force. This airplane [Śrīla Prabhupāda gestures toward a passing aircraft] is flying, but is it flying undirected?

DR. SINGH. Someone is directing it.

ŚRĪLA PRABHUPĀDA. Yes. Everything is working under someone's direction. Why do the rascal scientists deny this? The airplane is a big machine, but it is flying under the direction of a small spiritual spark, the pilot. Scientists cannot prove that this big 747 airplane could fly without the small spiritual spark. So, as the small spiritual spark can direct a large plane, the big spiritual spark directs the whole cosmic manifestation.

Setting the Real Problems Aside

ŚRĪLA PRABHUPĀDA. The *Śvetāśvatara Upaniṣad* says:

keśāgra-śata-bhāgasya
śatāṁśaḥ sādṛśātmakaḥ
jīvaḥ sūkṣma-svarūpo 'yaṁ
saṅkhyātīto hi cit-kaṇaḥ

According to this verse, the measurement of the soul, the proprietor of the body, is one ten-thousandth part of the tip of a hair. This is very small—atomic. But because of that atomic spiritual energy, my body is working. That atomic spiritual energy is within the body, and therefore the body works, and the airplane flies. Is it so difficult to understand?

Suppose a man thinks himself very stout and strong. *Why* is he stout and strong? It is only because within him there exists a spiritual spark. As soon as the small spiritual spark is gone, his strength and vigor disappear, and the vultures come and eat his body. If scientists say that matter is the cause and origin of life, then let us ask them to bring back to life just one dead man, one great man like Professor Einstein. Let them inject some chemicals so that just one dead man may come back to life and work again. But this they cannot do. There are so many things they do not know, but still they are called scientists.

DR. SINGH. Sometimes when a problem is too dreadfully serious, we tend to take it lightly.

ŚRĪLA PRABHUPĀDA. Yes. When a monkey confronts a tiger, the monkey closes its eyes, and the tiger immediately attacks. Similarly, if scientists cannot solve a problem, they may think, "All right, let it go on." This is actually what they are doing, because our real problem is death. No one wants to die, but scientists cannot stop death. They speak superficially about death because they cannot give any relief from it. We do not wish to die, we do not wish to become old, and we do not wish to become diseased. But what help can the scientists offer? They cannot do anything about it. They have set aside the major problems.

President Jackal

ŚRĪLA PRABHUPĀDA. In Bengal there is a story called *jaṅgal-kī rājā,* concerning a jackal who became king of the forest. Jackals are known for their cunning. One day this jackal came into a village and fell into a tub of blue dye. He fled to the forest, but he had become blue. So all the animals said, "What is this? What is this? Who is this animal?" Even the lion was surprised: "We have never seen you before, sir. So who are you?" The jackal replied, "I have been sent by God." So they began to worship him as God. But then one night some other jackals began to cry: "*Wa, wa, wa!*" And since jackals cannot restrain themselves from returning the call of their own kind, this blue jackal also began to cry, "*Wa, wa, wa!*" And thus he exposed himself before all the other animals as being nothing more than a jackal. Many jackals have been arrested and have resigned from your government.

BRAHMĀNANDA SVĀMĪ. The Watergate affair. It is called the Watergate scandal.

ŚRĪLA PRABHUPĀDA. Practically speaking, at the present moment no honest man can become a government official. This is true everywhere. Unless one is a rogue, a dishonest person, one cannot maintain his governmental position. Therefore no noble man goes into the government. But what can you do?

DR. SINGH. Politicians are the greatest cheaters.

ŚRĪLA PRABHUPĀDA. Yes, they are scoundrels. One philosopher said that politics is the last resort of scoundrels.

Science Should Stop Death

BRAHMĀNANDA SVĀMĪ. Do scientists know the cause of cancer?

DR. SINGH. They have several theories.

ŚRĪLA PRABHUPĀDA. Suppose you know the cause of cancer. What is the benefit? Even if you could stop cancer, you could not make a man live forever. That is not possible. Cancer or no cancer, a man has to die. He cannot stop death. Death may be caused, if not by cancer, simply by an accident. Real scientific research should aim at stopping death. That is real science, and that is Kṛṣṇa consciousness. Simply to discover some medicine to cure disease is not a triumph. The real triumph is to stop *all* disease. *Bhagavad-gītā* [8.16] asserts that the real trouble is birth, death, old age and disease. *Ābrahma-bhuvanāl lokāḥ punar āvartino 'rjuna:* "From the highest planet in the material world down to the lowest, all are places of misery wherein repeated birth and death take place." The solution to the problem of repeated birth and death is Kṛṣṇa consciousness, which we are practicing and offering to everyone. The perfect result of this practice is that after the present body becomes useless and dies, one is no longer forced to accept a material body subject to birth, death, disease and old age. This is *real* science.

The Sixth Morning Walk

Recorded on May 7, 1973,
on the shores of the Pacific Ocean near Los Angeles.

Śrīla Prabhupāda is accompanied by Dr. Singh, Brahmānanda Svāmī and other students.

Chemicals From Mystic Power

ŚRĪLA PRABHUPĀDA. The scientists say that life begins from chemicals. But the real question is, "Where have the chemicals come from?" The chemicals come from life, and this means that life has mystic powers. For example, an orange tree contains many oranges, and each orange contains chemicals—citric acid and others. So where have these chemicals come from? Obviously they have come from the life within the tree. The scientists are missing the origin of the chemicals. They have started their investigation from the chemicals, but they cannot identify the origin of the chemicals. Chemicals come from the supreme life—God. Just as the living body of a man produces many chemicals, the supreme life (the Supreme Lord) is producing all the chemicals found in the atmosphere, in the water, in humans, in animals and in the earth. And that is called mystic power. Unless the mystic power of the Lord is accepted, there is no solution to the problem of the origin of life.

DR. SINGH. The scientists will reply that they cannot believe in mystic power.

ŚRĪLA PRABHUPĀDA. But they must explain the origin of the chemicals. Anyone can see that an ordinary tree is producing many chemicals. But how does it produce them? Since the scientists cannot answer this, they must accept that the living force has mystic power. I cannot even explain how my fingernail is growing out of my finger; it is beyond the power of my brain. In other words, my fingernail is growing by inconceivable potency, *acintya-śakti.* So if *acintya-śakti* exists in an ordinary human being, imagine how much *acintya-śakti* God possesses.

The difference between God and me is that although I have the same potencies as God, I can produce only a small quantity of chemicals, whereas He can produce enormous quantities. I can produce a little water in the form of perspiration, but God can produce the seas. Analysis of one drop of seawater gives you the qualitative analysis of the sea, without any mistake. Similarly, the ordinary living being is part and parcel of God, so by analyzing the living beings we can begin to understand God. In God there is great mystic potency. God's mystic potency is working swiftly, exactly like an electric machine. Some machines operate by electrical energy, and they are so nicely made that all the work is done simply by pushing a button. Similarly, God said, "Let there be creation," and there was creation. Considered in this way, the workings of nature are not very difficult to understand. God has such wonderful potencies that the creation, on His order alone, immediately takes place.

BRAHMĀNANDA SVĀMĪ. Some scientists don't accept God or *acintya-śakti.*

ŚRĪLA PRABHUPĀDA. That is their rascaldom. God exists, and His *acintya-śakti* also exists. Where does a bird's power to fly come from? Both you and the bird are living entities, but the bird can fly because of its *acintya-śakti,* and you cannot. To give another example, semen is produced from blood. A man has mystic power in his body so that because he is sexually inclined, blood is transformed into semen. How is this done unless there is some mystic power involved? There are many mystic powers in the living entities. The cow eats grass and produces milk. Everyone knows this, but can you take some grass and produce milk? Can you? Therefore there is mystic power within the cow. As soon as the cow eats grass, she can transform it into milk. Men and women are basically the same, but as a man you cannot eat food and produce milk, although a woman can. These are mystic powers.

DR. SINGH. Scientists would say that there are different enzymes or chemicals inside different types of bodies and that these account for the cow's producing milk.

ŚRĪLA PRABHUPĀDA. Yes, but who produced those enzymes and that arrangement? That was done by mystic power. You cannot make these enzymes or that arrangement. You cannot produce milk from dry grass in your laboratory. Within your body, by mystic power, you can transform food into blood and tissue, but in your laboratory, without mystic power, you cannot even transform grass into milk. Therefore you must accept the existence of mystic power.

The Origin of Mystic Power

ŚRĪLA PRABHUPĀDA. *Yogīs* are mainly concerned with developing different mystic powers. A *yogī* can walk on the water without drowning. The law of gravity does not operate on him. That is a mystic power called *laghimā*. *Laghimā* means that a person can become lighter than cotton and counteract the law of gravity. The *yoga* system simply develops the inconceivable potency already present in the practitioner. These boys are swimming [gesturing to surf bathers], but I cannot swim. Yet that swimming power is potential within me; I simply have to practice it. So, if yogic power is so potent in the human being, think how much more yogic power God has. Therefore, in the *Vedas* He is called Yogeśvara, which means "master of all mystic power." In the *Bhagavad-gītā* [10.8] Kṛṣṇa says, *ahaṁ sarvasya prabhavo mattaḥ sarvaṁ pravartate:* "I am the source of all spiritual and material worlds. Everything emanates from Me." Unless we accept this statement from God, there is no conclusive explanation to the origin of material nature. God cannot be understood without accepting the existence of mystic power, but if you understand God scientifically, then you will understand everything.

DR. SINGH. So do you mean to say that science has started from an intermediate point—not from the original point?

ŚRĪLA PRABHUPĀDA. Yes, that is it exactly. They are ignorant of the origin. The scientists start from one point—but where does that point come from? That they do not know, in spite of vast research. One has to accept that the original source is God, who is full of all mystic powers and from whom everything emanates. He Himself says in the *Bhagavad-gītā, ahaṁ sarvasya prabhavo* *mattaḥ sarvaṁ pravartate:* "I am the source of all spiritual and material worlds. Everything emanates from Me." Our conclusions are not based on blind faith; they are most scientific. Matter comes from life. In life—in the origin—there are unlimited material resources; that is the great mystery of creation.

If you drop a needle, it will fall immediately, but a bird weighing several pounds can float in the air. We must establish the *origin* of this floating. If we study nature, we find that every living entity has some mystic power. A man cannot live within the water for more than a few hours, yet a fish lives there continuously. Is that not mystic power?

DR. SINGH. It is mystic power for me, but not for the fish.

ŚRĪLA PRABHUPĀDA. Yes. That is because mystic power is not uniformly distributed. But all the mystic powers exist in God, the origin of everything. I derive some of His mystic power, you derive some, and the birds derive some. But the storehouse of mystic power is God.

There are eight basic types of mystic powers. Some of them are *laghimā* (by which one can become lighter than a feather), *mahimā* (by which one can become bigger than a mountain), *prāpti* (which enables one to capture anything he likes) and *īśitva* (by which one can completely subdue and control another being). Another type of mystic power can be seen in the sun, because from the sunshine innumerable things are inexplicably produced. Unless the scientists accept the existence of mystic power, they cannot explain these phenomena. They are simply beating around the bush.

DR. SINGH. A clever scientist may say anything to prove his point, without actually proving it. A real scientist must reach the ultimate, original cause—the final analysis.

ŚRĪLA PRABHUPĀDA. Yes, unless he finds the ultimate source, he is not actually practicing science.

DR. SINGH. Does understanding mysticism mean knowing that every day our bodies are dying?

ŚRĪLA PRABHUPĀDA. Yes.

DR. SINGH. But the average man does not think he is dying.

ŚRĪLA PRABHUPĀDA. That is due to foolishness. Every moment he is dying, but he is thinking, "I shall live forever." Actually, death begins from the very moment of birth. Our analysis of the problem is that since people are dying, we should *stop* their death. But the so-called scientists are not only accelerating the process of death, but also refusing to take constructive advice to correct themselves.

The Seventh Morning Walk

Recorded on May 8, 1973,
on the shores of the Pacific Ocean near Los Angeles.

Śrīla Prabhupāda is accompanied by Dr. Singh and other students.

The Cheaters and the Cheated

ŚRĪLA PRABHUPĀDA. Natural phenomena such as the law of gravity or weightlessness are *acintya-śakti,* inconceivable energies, and real science means to understand this *acintya-śakti.* To observe a chain of events only from a certain point in time is unscientific and gives only incomplete knowledge. We must know where things *begin.* If we carry our investigation far enough, we will find that the origin of nature is *acintya-śakti.* For example, with brain, brush and color we can paint a flower. But we cannot conceive how vegetation throughout the whole earth is automatically growing and fructifying. We can explain the painted flower, but we cannot explain the real flower. Scientists actually cannot explain biological growth. They simply juggle words like *molecule* and *chromosome,* but they cannot actually explain the phenomena.

The essential fault of the so-called scientists is that they have adopted the inductive process to arrive at their conclusions. For example, if a scientist wants to determine by the inductive process whether or not man is mortal, he must study every man to try to discover if some or one of them may be immortal. The scientist says, "I cannot accept the proposition that all men are mortal. There may be some men who are immortal. I have not yet seen every man. Therefore how can I accept that man is mortal?" This is called the inductive process. And the deductive process means that your father, your teacher or your *guru* says that man is mortal, and you accept it.

DR. SINGH. So there is an ascending process of gaining knowledge and a descending process?[7]

ŚRĪLA PRABHUPĀDA. Yes. The ascending process will never be successful, because it relies on the information gathered through the senses, and the senses are imperfect. So we accept the descending process.

God cannot be known by the inductive process. Therefore He is called *adhokṣaja,* which means "unknowable by direct perception." The scientists say there is no God because they are trying to understand Him by direct perception. But He is *adhokṣaja*! Therefore, the scientists are ignorant of God because they are missing the method of knowing Him. In order to understand transcendental science, one must approach a bona fide spiritual master, hear from him submissively and render service to him. Lord Kṛṣṇa explains that in the *Bhagavad-gītā* [4.34]: *tad viddhi praṇipātena paripraśnena sevayā.*

My Guru Mahārāja[8] once said, "The modern world is a society of the cheaters and the cheated." Unfortunately, the cheated are eulogizing the cheaters, and the small cheaters are worshiping the great cheaters. Suppose a flock of asses comes and eulogizes me, saying, "Oh, you are Jagad-guru."[9] What is the value of their praise? But if a gentleman or learned man gives praise, his words have some value. Generally, however, the persons who are praising and those who are being praised are both ignorant. As the *Vedas* put it, *saṁstutaḥ puruṣaḥ paśuḥ:* "A big animal is being praised by a small animal."

Compassion

ŚRĪLA PRABHUPĀDA. The law is cheating, medical science is cheating, and the government is cheating. Top government officials are charged with taking bribes. If the governor takes bribes and the constable takes bribes, then where is the good society? People elect the leader who promises them happiness. But since that happiness is *māyā* [or illusion], he can never deliver it, and society simply becomes filled with cheaters. Since people are actually after this illusory happiness, however, they continue to elect such unscrupulous leaders time and time again.

The position of a Vaiṣṇava[10] is to take compassion on all these ignorant people. The great Vaiṣṇava Prahlāda Mahārāja once prayed to the Lord, "My Lord, as far as I am concerned, I have no problems. My consciousness is always absorbed in Your very powerful transcendental activities, and therefore I have understood things clearly. But I am deeply concerned for these rascals who are engaged in activities for illusory happiness."

A Vaiṣṇava thinks only about how people can become happy. He knows that they are vainly searching after something that will never come to be. For fifty or sixty years people search after illusory happiness, but then they must die without completing the work and without knowing what will happen after death. Actually, their position is like that of an animal, because an animal also does not know what happens to him after death. The animal does not know the value of life, nor why he has come here. By the influence of *māyā,* he simply eats, sleeps, mates, defends and dies. That's all. Throughout their lives the ignorant animals—and the animalistic men—greatly endeavor to do these five things only: eat, sleep, mate, defend and die. Therefore the business of a Vaiṣṇava is to instruct people that God exists, that we are His servants, and that we can enjoy an eternally blissful life serving Him and developing our love for Him.

Beyond the Cage

DR. SINGH. But doesn't the living entity need matter as long as he is in material nature?

ŚRĪLA PRABHUPĀDA. No, the living entity is purely spiritual; therefore, he doesn't require matter. Because his thinking is diseased, however, he believes he does. The conditioned living entity is like a drunkard who doesn't require drinking, but who nevertheless thinks, "Without drinking, I shall die." This is called *māyā,* or illusion. Is it true that if a drunkard doesn't get his drink, he will die?

DR. SINGH. No, but if a man doesn't eat, he will die.

ŚRĪLA PRABHUPĀDA. That's also not a fact. Last night we were discussing Raghunātha dāsa Gosvāmī.[11] In his later life, he almost completely abstained from eating and sleeping. He would drink only a little buttermilk every three or four days, and he worked twenty-two hours a day, sleeping two or three. And some days he did not sleep at all. So you may ask, "How could he survive?" Actually, he lived for one hundred years. Eating, sleeping, mating and defending were not problems for Raghunātha dāsa Gosvāmī, but still he lived. Because he was a pure devotee of Kṛṣṇa, he was fully aware that the soul is eternal and independent, although it has been put into this bodily cage, which it actually does not require. Suppose a bird is encaged. Is he living simply because he is in the cage? Without the cage he is free. People are thinking that by being encaged within the body they are happy. That is nonsense. Actually, our encagement within this body makes us fearful. But as soon as we purify our existence—we do not even have to come out of our bodies—we will immediately be *abhaya,* fearless.

brahma-bhūtaḥ prasannātmā
na śocati na kāṅkṣati
samaḥ sarveṣu bhūteṣu
mad-bhaktiṁ labhate parām[12]

We can immediately awaken to our original, spiritual existence, in which there is no more fear, no more lamentation, and no more material desire.

DR. SINGH. But the scientist would still want some more explanations as to how the living entity can be independent of matter.

ŚRĪLA PRABHUPĀDA. As long as you are conditioned, you are dependent on matter. For example, a man from Africa is conditioned because he cannot tolerate this cold weather. Therefore he feels discomfort. But there are many people here [gesturing toward children playing on the beach] who are not affected by the cold. The ability to tolerate is simply a question of conditioning.

When you are conditioned, you think in terms of dualities like hot and cold, pain and pleasure. But when you are liberated, you have no such conditioned thoughts. Spiritual life means to become unconditioned—to come to the *brahma-bhūta* stage. That is the perfection of life. Being conditioned means that although the living entity is eternal, due to his conditioning he thinks that he is born, he is dying, he is diseased and he is old. But an unconditioned person is not even old. Kṛṣṇa is described in the *Brahma-saṁhitā* as *advaitam acyutam anādim ananta-rūpam ādyaṁ purāṇa-puruṣaṁ nava-yauvanaṁ ca.* This means that He is the oldest person, the first person, but that He has no old age. He always appears just like a young man of twenty because He is fully spiritual.

The Eighth Morning Walk

Recorded on May 11, 1973,
on the shores of the Pacific Ocean near Los Angeles.

Śrīla Prabhupāda is accompanied by Dr. Singh and other students.

The Evolution of Consciousness

DR. SINGH. Śrīla Prabhupāda, I came across a statement in the *Bhagavad-gītā* to the effect that all 8,400,000 species of living entities are created simultaneously. Is that correct?

ŚRĪLA PRABHUPĀDA. Yes.

DR. SINGH. Does that mean that there are some living entities who come directly to the human species without undergoing the evolutionary process?

ŚRĪLA PRABHUPĀDA. Yes. Living beings move from one bodily form to another. The forms already exist. The living entity simply transfers himself, just as a man transfers himself from one apartment to another. One apartment is first class, another is second class and another is third class. Suppose a person comes from a lower-class apartment to a first-class apartment. The person is the same, but now, according to his capacity for payment, or *karma,*[13] he is able to occupy a higher-class apartment. Real evolution does not mean physical development, but development of consciousness. Do you follow?

DR. SINGH. I think so. Do you mean that if one falls to one of the lower stages of life, he must evolve step by step up to the higher stages?

ŚRĪLA PRABHUPĀDA. Yes. As you get more money you can move to a better apartment. The apartment already exists, however. It is not that the lower-class apartment *becomes* the higher-class apartment. That is Darwin's nonsensical theory. He would say that the apartment has become high class. Modern scientists think that life has come from matter. They say that millions and millions of years ago there was simply matter, but no life. We do not accept that. Of the two energies—life and matter—life, or spirit, is the original, superior energy, and matter is the resultant inferior energy.

DR. SINGH. Do they exist simultaneously?

ŚRĪLA PRABHUPĀDA. Yes, but spirit is independent, and matter is dependent. For example, I can live even without my hands or legs. If they were amputated, I could survive. Therefore I am not dependent on my hands and legs; my hands and legs are dependent on me, the spirit soul within my body.

Bodies for Eternal Desires

DR. SINGH. But do life and matter come simultaneously?

ŚRĪLA PRABHUPĀDA. No. They do not "come" at all. They already exist. The "coming" idea is in our minds because we are living in this limited world, where we see that there is a beginning to everything. Therefore we think in terms of things "coming." But actually matter and spirit already exist. When I am born, I think my birth is the beginning of the world. But the world already exists. Another example is a fire. When you light a fire, do the light and heat begin later on? No. Whenever a fire is ignited, immediately there is light and heat. But suppose I think, "Now there is a fire, but I have to wait for the light and heat to come later on." Isn't that foolishness?

DR. SINGH. But fire is the source of the heat and light.

ŚRĪLA PRABHUPĀDA. Yes, but still the heat and light exist simultaneously with the fire. Similarly, the eternal living entities have many different eternal desires. And all the varieties of species also exist eternally to fit these various eternal desires.

DR. SINGH. And the living entities are made to live in different bodies according to these desires?

ŚRĪLA PRABHUPĀDA. Yes. For example, the government constructs a prison house because it knows there will be criminals. So when a criminal is tried and convicted, the prison already exists, even before the judgment period. Similarly, God is described as *sarva-jña,* He who knows everything. Thus He knows that some living entities will become criminal and rebel against His service. Furthermore, He knows the various desires the living entities in the material world acquire according to the three modes of material nature. Therefore He creates all the species of life from the very beginning to accommodate all the conditioned souls.

The three modes of material nature are *sattva-guṇa* [goodness], *rajo-guṇa* [passion] and *tamo-guṇa* [ignorance]. With these three qualities, all the different objects of the material world are made, just as one might mix the three primary colors (blue, red and yellow) to make millions of hues. The great expertise required to handle this arrangement exists in nature. According to the *Bhagavad-gītā* [3.27], *prakṛteḥ kriyamāṇāni guṇaiḥ karmāṇi sarvaśaḥ:* "All activities are performed by the modes of material nature." And these modes are manifested in the different types of species, which include plants, trees, aquatics, human beings, demigods, cats, dogs and many others, totaling 8,400,000.

The Supreme Lord expands Himself as the Paramātmā, or Supersoul, in everyone's heart. Although dwelling in the material body, this Supersoul is not material, even though He is the original source of the material body. Because heat and light are the energies of the sun, the sun never feels "too hot." Similarly, for the Paramātmā there is no distinction between spiritual and material because both the material and the spiritual energies emanate from Him. Sometimes we see that clouds cover the sun; but that is actually our imperfection. We on this planet experience both sunshine and cloudiness, but on the sun, even though it can create clouds, only sunshine is experienced. Similarly, the division of matter and spirit is our experience, not God's. Whether He comes in a so-called material body or in a spiritual body, He is always spiritual. For Him matter and spirit are the same because He is the energetic. He can turn matter into spirit, and spirit into matter.

H_2O Plus Mystic Power

DR. SINGH. The chemists and the scientists think that certain elements enable the spirit soul to remain in the material world. These elements, they say, are carbon, hydrogen, nitrogen and oxygen—the main elements that combine to form living units. I think the *Vedas* teach that in order for a living creature to develop, spirit must first enter within these preexisting chemical elements. Is that correct?

ŚRĪLA PRABHUPĀDA. Yes. For example, the earth contains everything necessary for a plant to grow, but you must first put a seed in the earth. Similarly, a mother has within her womb all the necessary ingredients for creating another body, but the father must first inject the semen, or seed, into the womb; then the child will develop. A dog forms a dog's body, and a human forms a human body. Why? Because all the required ingredients are there, respectively.

We find a certain quantity of chemicals in my body, a smaller quantity in an ant's body, and a greater quantity in an elephant's body. So, if I can create so many more chemicals than an ant, and an elephant can create so many more chemicals than I can, then just think how many more chemicals God can create! *This* is the basis on which scientists should consider how hydrogen and oxygen combine to form water. Otherwise, they cannot identify the source of the vast quantities of hydrogen and oxygen required to make the oceans. But we can. This hydrogen and oxygen exist in the *virāṭ-rūpa,* the universal body of the Lord. Why do the scientists fail to understand this plain truth? Hydrogen and oxygen combine to form the water in the seas. We both accept this fact. But the scientists are surprised to hear that the origin of this huge quantity of hydrogen and oxygen is actually *acintya-śakti,* or the inconceivable mystic power of the Lord.

The Definition of "Life"

DR. SINGH. I have noticed a disagreement within the scientific community over the definition of *living* and *nonliving.* Some say that if a being can reproduce, it is alive. Therefore, they claim to have created life because certain large DNA molecules[14] produced in the laboratory can replicate themselves; that is, they can reproduce other chains of molecules by their own power. Some scientists say these DNA molecules are living, and others say they are not.

ŚRĪLA PRABHUPĀDA. Because somebody is saying one thing and somebody is saying another, their knowledge must be imperfect.

DR. SINGH. Can we define *living* as "containing consciousness" and *nonliving* as "without consciousness"?

ŚRĪLA PRABHUPĀDA. Yes, that is the difference. As Kṛṣṇa says in the *Bhagavad-gītā* [2.17], *avināśi tu tad viddhi yena sarvam idaṁ tatam:* "That which is spread all over the body is indestructible." Anyone can understand what is spread all over a living body; it is consciousness. According to our consciousness at the time of death, we are awarded a particular bodily shape. If you have a dog's consciousness, you will get a dog's body, and if you have a godly consciousness, you will get a demigod's body.[15] Kṛṣṇa gives everyone the freedom to take whatever body he wants:

yānti deva-vratā devān
pitṝn yānti pitṛ-vratāḥ
bhūtāni yānti bhūtejyā
yānti mad-yājino 'pi mām

"Those who worship the demigods will take birth among the demigods; those who worship ghosts and spirits will take birth among such beings; those who worship ancestors go to the ancestors; and those who worship Me will live with Me." [Bg. 9.25]

Darwin Condemned

DR. SINGH. If a human being doesn't attain liberation, does he have to pass through all 8,400,000 species of life before again coming to the human form?

ŚRĪLA PRABHUPĀDA. No, only in the lower forms of life does the living entity progress step by step, according to the laws of nature. In the human form of life, he is endowed with developed consciousness—he has discretion. Therefore if he is advanced in consciousness, he is not going to get the body of a dog or cat; he will get another human body.

prāpya puṇya-kṛtāṁ lokān
uṣitvā śāśvatīḥ samāḥ
śucīnāṁ śrīmatāṁ gehe
yoga-bhraṣṭo 'bhijāyate[16]

The word *yoga-bhraṣṭaḥ* refers to someone practicing *yoga* who somehow or other could not fully succeed. There's no question of evolution here; he is again awarded a human body. He does not get a cat's body or a dog's body. As with the apartments we were discussing, if you can pay more, you get a nicer apartment. You do not have to come to the lower-class apartment first.

DR. SINGH. What you have been saying completely contradicts Darwin's theory of evolution.

ŚRĪLA PRABHUPĀDA. Darwin is a rascal. What is his theory? We kick out Darwin's philosophy. The more we kick out Darwin's philosophy, the more we advance in spiritual consciousness.

DR. SINGH. Many scientists doubt Darwin's theories. But Darwin's supporters say that life started from matter and evolved from unicellular organisms to multicellular organisms. They believe that higher species like animals and men did not exist at the beginning of creation.

ŚRĪLA PRABHUPĀDA. Darwin and his followers are rascals. If originally there were no higher species, why do they exist now? Also, why do the lower species still exist? For example, at the present moment we see both the intellectual person and the foolish ass. Why do both these entities exist simultaneously? Why hasn't the ass form evolved upward and disappeared? Why do we never see a monkey giving birth to a human? The Darwinists' theory that human life began in such and such an era is nonsense. *Bhagavad-gītā* says that you can directly transmigrate to any species of life you like, according to your efforts. Sometimes I travel to America, sometimes to Australia and sometimes to Africa. The countries already exist. I am simply traveling through them. It is not that because I have come to America, I have *created* or *become* America. And there are many countries I have not yet seen. Does that mean they do not exist? The scientists who support Darwin are nonsensical. *Bhagavad-gītā* clearly says that all the species exist simultaneously, and that you can go to whichever species you like. You can even go up to the kingdom of God, if you so desire. All this is declared in *Bhagavad-gītā* by Lord Kṛṣṇa.

The Ninth Morning Walk

Recorded on May 13, 1973,
in Cheviot Hills Park, Los Angeles.

Śrīla Prabhupāda is accompanied by Dr. Singh, Karandhara dāsa adhikārī and other students.

Evolution From Human to Dog

ŚRĪLA PRABHUPĀDA. The so-called scientists are putting their faith in a fraudulent theory. Kṛṣṇa says, *ahaṁ sarvasya prabhavaḥ:* "I am the origin of everything." [Bg. 10.8] Kṛṣṇa is life; Kṛṣṇa is not a dead stone.

DR. SINGH. So matter is caused by life?

ŚRĪLA PRABHUPĀDA. Yes, and matter grows upon life; my body grows upon me, the spirit soul. For example, I have put on this overcoat, which is made according to the size of my body. But I would be foolish if I thought, "I am this overcoat."

STUDENT. Śrīla Prabhupāda, mineralogists have proven that mountains are growing by sedimentary activity. Is this growth due to the presence of the spirit soul?

ŚRĪLA PRABHUPĀDA. Yes. *Śrīmad-Bhāgavatam* describes mountains as the bones of God, and the grass as the hair on His body. So, in this sense, God has the biggest body.

DR. SINGH. Śrīla Prabhupāda, what is the difference between the transmigration of souls in animal bodies and the transmigration of human souls?

ŚRĪLA PRABHUPĀDA. Animals transmigrate in only one direction—upward—but human beings can transmigrate to either a higher or a lower form of life. The body is awarded according to the living entity's desire. The lower animals have one kind of desire, but the human being has thousands and millions of desires—animal desires as well as human desires. By nature's law, the lower species are coming up from animal forms to the higher, human forms. But once you come to the human form, if you don't cultivate Kṛṣṇa consciousness you may return to the body of a cat or dog.

Nirvāṇa

DR. SINGH. The scientists have no information that there is evolution up *or* down from the human platform.

ŚRĪLA PRABHUPĀDA. Therefore I say they are rascals. They have no knowledge, yet they still claim to be scientists. Real science is in the *Bhagavad-gītā,* where Kṛṣṇa says, *yānti deva-vratā devān pitṝn yānti pitṛ-vratāḥ* [Bg. 9.25]. This means that whatever one worships in this life will determine the type of body he gets in his next life. But if one worships Kṛṣṇa, he ends the process of transmigration entirely. *Yaṁ prāpya na nivartante tad dhāma:* "When one goes to that supreme abode of Mine, he never returns [to this material world of birth and death]." [Bg. 8.21] Promotion to the spiritual world (*saṁsiddhiṁ paramām*) is the ultimate perfection of human life. Read *Bhagavad-gītā;* everything is there. But the scientists have no idea of this perfection; they do not even believe in the existence of the living entity apart from the gross body.

DR. SINGH. They do not speak of the living entity; they speak only of bodies.

STUDENT. Their conception is something akin to Buddhism. The Buddhists say that the body is like a house. Just as a house is put together with wood, the body is put together with chemicals. And when the body dies, it is just like a house that falls apart. Just as the house becomes simply pieces of wood and then there is no more house, so the body becomes simply chemicals and there is no more body and no more life.

ŚRĪLA PRABHUPĀDA. That state is called *nirvāṇa.* And then, with the ingredients, you can build another house or another body. That is Buddhism. The Buddhists do not have any information regarding the soul.

Destiny and Karma

STUDENT. Some scientists argue that there are several souls within each body. They use the earthworm as an example. If you cut it in half, both parts will live. They say this proves that two souls occupied the original worm's body.

ŚRĪLA PRABHUPĀDA. No. It is simply that a new soul has come to occupy the other half of the worm's body.

DR. SINGH. Must the spirit soul necessarily have a body—either spiritual or material?

ŚRĪLA PRABHUPĀDA. The soul already has a spiritual body, which the material body covers. My material body grows upon me—my spiritual body—but my material body is unnatural. The real body is spiritual. I am accepting various bodies that are unnatural to my constitution. My real, constitutional position is to be the servant of Kṛṣṇa. As long as I do not come to that position, I remain a servant of matter and get many material bodies according to the laws of material energy. I get one body and then give it up. I desire something else and again get another body. This process is going on under the strict laws of material nature. People think they completely control their destinies, but they are always under nature's law of *karma:*

prakṛteḥ kriyamāṇāni
guṇaiḥ karmāṇi sarvaśaḥ
ahaṅkāra-vimūḍhātmā
kartāham iti manyate

"The bewildered spirit soul, under the influence of the three modes of material nature, thinks himself to be the doer of activities that are in actuality carried out by nature." [Bg. 3.27] The source of this bewilderment is that the living entity thinks, "I am this body."

īśvaraḥ sarva-bhūtānāṁ
hṛd-deśe 'rjuna tiṣṭhati
bhrāmayan sarva-bhūtāni
yantrārūḍhāni māyayā[17]

In this verse the word *yantra,* or "machine," means that in any species of life, we are traveling in bodies that are like machines provided by material nature. Sometimes we are moving to higher species, sometimes to lower species. But if, by the mercy of the spiritual master and Kṛṣṇa, one gets the seed of devotional service and cultivates it, he can become free from the cycle of birth and death. Then his life is successful. Otherwise, he has to travel up and down the different species of life, becoming sometimes a blade of grass, sometimes a lion, and so forth.

Advertising Ignorance as Knowledge

STUDENT. So it is our desire to enjoy that causes us to take on these material bodies, and our desire to achieve Kṛṣṇa that brings us to our natural position?

ŚRĪLA PRABHUPĀDA. Yes.

DR. SINGH. But there seems to be a constant struggle with our lower nature. We are constantly fighting our desires for sense gratification, even though we want to serve Kṛṣṇa. Does this continue?

STUDENT. The body is almost like a dictator from within.

ŚRĪLA PRABHUPĀDA. Yes. That means you are strongly under the control of material energy, or *māyā*.

DR. SINGH. Even though we also desire to serve Kṛṣṇa?

ŚRĪLA PRABHUPĀDA. Yes. A thief may know that if he steals he will be arrested and put into jail—he may have even seen others being arrested—yet he still steals. Even though he is aware that he is under the authority of the state, he still acts according to his desires. This is called *tamas*, or ignorance. Therefore, knowledge is the beginning of spiritual life. In *Bhagavad-gītā*, Kṛṣṇa gives Arjuna knowledge. He teaches, "You are not this body." This is the beginning of knowledge. But where is the university that teaches this knowledge? Dr. Singh, can you tell me where that university is that teaches this knowledge?

DR. SINGH. There is none.

ŚRĪLA PRABHUPĀDA. That is the position of education: there is no knowledge. They simply advertise ignorance as knowledge.

DR. SINGH. But if the scientists knew that they were not their bodies, their whole outlook would change.

ŚRĪLA PRABHUPĀDA. Yes, we want that.

STUDENT. But they don't want to admit their failure.

ŚRĪLA PRABHUPĀDA. Then that is further foolishness. If you are a fool and you pose yourself as intelligent, that is further foolishness. Then you cannot make progress. And if you remain in ignorance and advertise yourself as a man of knowledge, you are a great cheater. You are cheating yourself and cheating others. People are so mad after the material advancement of civilization that they have become exactly like cats and dogs. For instance, they have set up an immigration department, and as soon as you enter a country these dogs go, "Woof, woof, woof! Why have you come? What is your business?" This is a watchdog's activity. A first-class gentleman is being searched for a revolver. People cannot be trusted, and now there are so many educated rogues and thieves. So what is the meaning of advancement? Can we say that education means advancement? Is this civilization?

Fighting Ignorance With Arguments and Knowledge

STUDENT. Some people say that one reason for the Vietnam war was that the Communists were atheists. It was a dispute between the theists and the atheists. At least that is one excuse given for the war.

ŚRĪLA PRABHUPĀDA. We are also prepared to kill the atheists. But that killing is by preaching. If I kill your ignorance, it can also be called killing. Killing doesn't necessarily mean that everyone has to take the sword.

DR. SINGH. A new method of warfare?

ŚRĪLA PRABHUPĀDA. No, fighting ignorance with arguments and knowledge has always existed. The bodily conception of life is animal life. The animal does not know about matter and spirit. And one who is under the bodily conception of life is no better than an animal. When an animal "talks," the intelligent man laughs. Such "talk" is nonsense. The animal is not talking knowledge.

STUDENT. At least the animals live by certain codes. They do not kill unnecessarily, and they only eat when necessary, whereas humans kill unnecessarily and eat unnecessarily. So in one sense humans are lower than animals.

ŚRĪLA PRABHUPĀDA. Therefore we must suffer more than animals. Kṛṣṇa consciousness is not a bogus, sentimental religious movement. It is a scientific movement designed to alleviate human suffering.

DR. SINGH. Scientists and other people say that everything in the universe is happening by chance.

ŚRĪLA PRABHUPĀDA. So, are they also writing books on the subject by chance?

KARANDHARA. The books are also written by chance, they say.

ŚRĪLA PRABHUPĀDA. So, what is their credit? By chance, anything can be written.

DR. SINGH. The French scientist Dr. J. Monod got the Nobel Prize in 1965. He says that everything started by chance—that by chance certain chemicals combined and formed the basic molecules.

ŚRĪLA PRABHUPĀDA. But where did the chemicals come from?

DR. SINGH. According to him, they were created simply by chance, and when the necessity arose, molecules of the chemicals reorientated themselves.

ŚRĪLA PRABHUPĀDA. If everything was happening by chance, how can there be necessity? How can he speak of chance and necessity in the same breath? It is nonsense. If everything is directed by chance, why do people send their children to school? Why not let them grow up by chance? Suppose I break a law. If I say, "Well, it just happened by chance," will I be excused?

DR. SINGH. So, is crime caused by ignorance?

ŚRĪLA PRABHUPĀDA. Yes. *That* is the cause: my ignorance.

STUDENT. It would certainly be stupid to say that a beautiful instrument like a violin was made by chance.

ŚRĪLA PRABHUPĀDA. Yes. It is most regrettable that such a rascal can get recognition. He is talking foolishness and getting recognition.

The Tenth Morning Walk

Recorded on May 14, 1973,
in Cheviot Hills Park, Los Angeles.

Śrīla Prabhupāda is accompanied by Dr. Singh and other students.

The Scientists' Mistake

ŚRĪLA PRABHUPĀDA. The scientists' mistake is that they are ignorant of the two energies—material and spiritual. They say that everything is material and that everything emanates from matter. The defect in their theories is that they begin from matter instead of spirit. Since matter comes from spirit, in a sense everything is spiritual. Spiritual energy is the source and can exist without the material energy. But the material energy has no existence without the spiritual energy. It is correct to say that darkness begins from light, not that light begins from darkness. Scientists think that consciousness comes from matter. Actually, consciousness always exists, but when it is covered or degraded by ignorance, it is a form of unconsciousness.

So "material" means forgetfulness of Kṛṣṇa, and "spiritual" means full consciousness of Kṛṣṇa. Is this clear? Try to understand: darkness comes from light. When no light is visible, then we are in darkness. Clouds are not to be found in the sun; that would be against the nature of the sun. But by the *energy* of the sun other things are temporarily created, such as mist, clouds or darkness. These creations are temporary, but the sun remains. Similarly, material nature is temporary, but spiritual nature is permanent. Kṛṣṇa consciousness means getting out of this temporary nature and attaining a permanent, spiritual nature. No one actually wants this temporary nature; no one likes this cloudy atmosphere.

DR. SINGH. Is this cloudy consciousness created from spiritual energy?

ŚRĪLA PRABHUPĀDA. Yes.

DR. SINGH. And matter is also created from the superior energy?

ŚRĪLA PRABHUPĀDA. *Ahaṁ sarvasya prabhavo mattaḥ sarvaṁ pravartate.* Kṛṣṇa says, "I am the source of all spiritual and material worlds. Everything emanates from Me." [Bg. 10.8] Kṛṣṇa is the creator of everything, bad or good. Actually, "bad and good" is a material creation. Kṛṣṇa's creation is good; God is good. What you think is bad is good for God. Therefore, we cannot understand Kṛṣṇa. He is doing something that in our consideration may be bad, but for Him there is no such thing as good or bad. For example, Kṛṣṇa married sixteen thousand wives. Some people may criticize, "Ah, He is so mad after women." But they do not see the whole picture. Kṛṣṇa's power is so great that He expanded Himself into sixteen thousand different husbands.

"Everything Is One" Is Nonsense

DR. SINGH. You said this mist of material nature is temporary. But why should we bother to disentangle ourselves from something transitory?

ŚRĪLA PRABHUPĀDA. Why do you put coverings on your body? You may walk naked. The weather will clear in a few hours. Why do you cover yourself?

DR. SINGH. The danger is now.

ŚRĪLA PRABHUPĀDA. Whenever it may be, why do you take this step of covering your body?

DR. SINGH. To avoid discomfort.

ŚRĪLA PRABHUPĀDA. Yes. Otherwise you would be uncomfortable. Not to bother to dress is the Māyāvāda theory: "Everything will come automatically, so why bother? Everything is one." That is a nonsensical theory. The Māyāvāda philosophy is that God is one and that every thing and every living being is equal to God.

We have no quarrel with the chemists if they begin from life, but unfortunately they say that everything begins from darkness—dead matter. That is what we object to. We say, "Begin from life," and they say, "No, begin from matter—darkness." The reason they are in darkness is simple: if one goes from darkness to light, he thinks that darkness is the beginning. Suppose you have been in darkness all your life, and now you suddenly come into the light. You will think, "Oh, light has come from darkness." Actually, darkness occurs when light becomes dim. Darkness does not produce light.

DR. SINGH. Then darkness is dependent on light?

ŚRĪLA PRABHUPĀDA. Yes. Or in other words, in the light there is no darkness. When the light is dim—then we experience darkness. Similarly, when our spiritual consciousness, or Kṛṣṇa consciousness, is dim, our consciousness is material.

In the morning we awaken, and at the end of the day we become tired and go to sleep. When life is somehow or other interrupted, we sleep. We sleep at night, and when we get up in the morning we understand that our wakefulness, or "life," has not come into existence from the sleepy condition. I was alive even while I slept, and on awakening I am still alive. This should be clearly understood. A baby comes from the womb of his mother. He thinks that his life has begun from the day he comes out of the womb. But that is not a fact. Actually, he is eternal. He constructed his material body within the womb of his mother while he was unconscious, and as soon as his bodily features were sufficiently developed, he came out of the womb and again to consciousness.

DR. SINGH. And he again falls asleep at death.

ŚRĪLA PRABHUPĀDA. Yes. That is described in *Bhagavad-gītā* [8.19]:

bhūta-grāmaḥ sa evāyaṁ
bhūtvā bhūtvā pralīyate
rātry-āgame 'vaśaḥ pārtha
prabhavaty ahar-āgame

"Again and again the day comes, and this host of beings is active, and again night falls, O Pārtha, and they are helplessly dissolved."

We Are Not These Bodies

ŚRĪLA PRABHUPĀDA. Do you see this flower? It has come back to consciousness, and soon it will dry up and die. This is material life. But spiritual life means to flower only—no dissolution. That is the difference between matter and spirit. I have achieved this body according to my consciousness in my last life. And I will receive my next body according to my consciousness in this life. This is also confirmed in the *Bhagavad-gītā* [8.6]:

yaṁ yaṁ vāpi smaran bhāvaṁ
tyajaty ante kalevaram
taṁ tam evaiti kaunteya
sadā tad-bhāva-bhāvitaḥ

"Whatever state of being one remembers when he quits his body, that state he will attain without fail."

DR. SINGH. Śrīla Prabhupāda, if our next body is always achieved by our consciousness in this life, how is it that I cannot remember my previous life?

ŚRĪLA PRABHUPĀDA. Do you remember everything you did last year, or even yesterday?

DR. SINGH. No, I don't.

ŚRĪLA PRABHUPĀDA. That is your nature: you forget.

DR. SINGH. *Some* things.

ŚRĪLA PRABHUPĀDA. And somebody forgets more than others. But we all forget.

DR. SINGH. Is that a principle of material nature?

ŚRĪLA PRABHUPĀDA. Yes. It is something like stealing. Somebody is a pickpocket and somebody is a bank robber, but both of them are stealing.

DR. SINGH. When we dream, are we being carried away by the subtle elements?

ŚRĪLA PRABHUPĀDA. You are being carried away by nature. Kṛṣṇa says in *Bhagavad-gītā* [3.27]:

prakṛteḥ kriyamāṇāni
guṇaiḥ karmāṇi sarvaśaḥ
ahaṅkāra-vimūḍhātmā
kartāham iti manyate

"The bewildered spirit soul, under the influence of the three modes of material nature, thinks himself to be the doer of activities that are in actuality carried out by nature." We forget our real identity because we are under the grip of material nature.

The first lesson in spiritual life is that we are not these bodies, but eternal spirit souls. Once you were a child. Now you are a grown man. Where is your childhood body? That body does not exist, but you still exist because you are eternal. The circumstantial body has changed, but *you* have not changed. This is the proof of eternality. You remember that you did certain things yesterday and certain things today, but you forget other things. Your body of yesterday is not today's body. Do you admit it or not? You cannot say that today is the thirteenth of May, 1973. You cannot say that today is yesterday. The thirteenth was yesterday. The day has changed. But *you* remember yesterday; and that *remembrance* is evidence of your eternality. The body has changed, but you remember it; therefore you are eternal, although the body is temporary. This proof is very simple. Even a child can understand it. Is it difficult to understand?

Changing Bodies

DR. SINGH. People want more proof.

ŚRĪLA PRABHUPĀDA. What more is required? The eternality of the soul is a simple fact. I am an eternal soul. My body is changing, but *I* am not changing. For example, I am now an old man. Sometimes I think, "Oh, I used to jump and play, but now I cannot jump because my body has changed." I *want* to jump, but I cannot do it. That jumping propensity is eternal, but because of my old body I cannot do it.

DR. SINGH. Opponents will say that according to their observation, the nature of consciousness is that it lasts for only one body.

ŚRĪLA PRABHUPĀDA. That is foolishness. In *Bhagavad-gītā* [2.13] Kṛṣṇa explains:

dehino 'smin yathā dehe
kaumāraṁ yauvanaṁ jarā
tathā dehāntara-prāptir
dhīras tatra na muhyati

"As the embodied soul continually passes, in this body, from boyhood to youth to old age, the soul similarly passes into another body at death. The self-realized soul is not bewildered by such a change." Just as this body is always changing (as I can see in my daily experience), there is a similar change at the time of death.

DR. SINGH. But according to the scientists, we cannot actually *observe* this last change.

ŚRĪLA PRABHUPĀDA. Their eyes are so imperfect that they cannot observe many, many things. Their ignorance does not make the *Bhagavad-gītā* unscientific. Why don't the scientists admit the imperfection of their senses? They must first admit the imperfection of their senses. Their seeing power does not determine what is and what is not science. Dogs cannot understand the laws of nature. Does that mean the laws of nature don't exist?

DR. SINGH. Well, the scientists admit that argument, but they say the way to become perfect is through objective information and experience.

ŚRĪLA PRABHUPĀDA. No. That is not the way to become perfect. No one can become perfect through imperfect thinking, and our thinking must be imperfect because our senses and minds are imperfect.

DR. SINGH. Śrīla Prabhupāda, another question can be raised. Is it not possible that the soul may accept three, four or five bodies and then die?

ŚRĪLA PRABHUPĀDA. You are accepting millions of bodies. I say that your body of yesterday is not your body of today. So, if you live for one hundred years, how many times have you changed bodies? Just calculate.

DR. SINGH. Thirteen.

ŚRĪLA PRABHUPĀDA. Why thirteen?

DR. SINGH. Medical science says that all the bodily cells are replaced every seven years.

ŚRĪLA PRABHUPĀDA. No, not every seven years—*every second.* Every second, the blood corpuscles are changing. Is it not so?

DR. SINGH. Yes.

ŚRĪLA PRABHUPĀDA. And as soon as the blood corpuscles change, you change your body.

DR. SINGH. In scientific terminology, can the eternality of the soul be compared to conservation of energy?

ŚRĪLA PRABHUPĀDA. There is no question of the *conservation* of energy, because energy is always existing.

DR. SINGH. But according to scientific terminology, the law of conservation of energy is that energy cannot be created or destroyed, which means, I think, that it is eternal.

ŚRĪLA PRABHUPĀDA. Oh, yes, that we admit. Kṛṣṇa is eternal; therefore all His energies are eternal.

DR. SINGH. Is that why the living entity is also eternal?

ŚRĪLA PRABHUPĀDA. Yes. If the sun is eternal, its energies—heat and light—are also eternal.

DR. SINGH. Does it follow from this, then, that life cannot be created or destroyed?

ŚRĪLA PRABHUPĀDA. Yes. Life is eternal. It is not created or destroyed. It is only temporarily covered. I am eternal, but last night I was covered by sleep, so I think in terms of yesterday and today. This is the condition of the material world.

Everything Is Spiritual

DR. SINGH. Is material consciousness the absence of Kṛṣṇa consciousness?

ŚRĪLA PRABHUPĀDA. Yes.

DR. SINGH. And when there is Kṛṣṇa consciousness, where is material nature?

ŚRĪLA PRABHUPĀDA. If you continue in Kṛṣṇa consciousness, you will see that nothing is material. When you offer a flower to Kṛṣṇa, it is not material. Kṛṣṇa will not accept anything material. And this does not mean that the flower is material on the bush, and then it becomes spiritual when you offer it to Kṛṣṇa. No. The flower is "material" only as long as you think that it is made for your enjoyment. But as soon as you see that it is for Kṛṣṇa's enjoyment, you see it as it really is—spiritual.

DR. SINGH. So the entire world is actually spiritual?

ŚRĪLA PRABHUPĀDA. Yes. Therefore, we want to engage everything in Kṛṣṇa's service; that is the spiritual world.

DR. SINGH. Can we also appreciate Kṛṣṇa's creation in that light? For example, can we think, "This tree is very beautiful because it is Kṛṣṇa's property"?

ŚRĪLA PRABHUPĀDA. Yes. That is Kṛṣṇa consciousness.

DR. SINGH. If someone looks at the Deity of Kṛṣṇa in the temple and thinks that it is only stone or wood, what does that mean?

ŚRĪLA PRABHUPĀDA. He is ignorant of the facts. How can the Deity be material? Stone is also Kṛṣṇa's energy. Just as electric energy is everywhere but only the electricians know how to utilize it, so Kṛṣṇa is everywhere—even in stone—but only His devotees know how to utilize stone to appreciate Kṛṣṇa. The devotees know that stone cannot exist outside of Kṛṣṇa. Therefore, when the devotees see the Deity, they say, "Here is Kṛṣṇa." They see the real oneness of Kṛṣṇa and His energy.

Simultaneously One and Different

DR. SINGH. Is it true that Kṛṣṇa conscious persons perceive Kṛṣṇa in a plain stone as much as in the Deity carved from stone?

ŚRĪLA PRABHUPĀDA. Yes.

DR. SINGH. Just as much?

ŚRĪLA PRABHUPĀDA. Yes. Why not? In the *Bhagavad-gītā* [9.4] Kṛṣṇa says:

mayā tatam idaṁ sarvaṁ
jagad avyakta-mūrtinā
mat-sthāni sarva-bhūtāni
na cāhaṁ teṣv avasthitaḥ

This means that Kṛṣṇa's energy—that is, Kṛṣṇa in His partially manifested form—pervades every atom of the universe. But His fully manifested personal form is present in the Deity shaped according to His directions. This is the philosophy of *acintya-bhedābheda-tattva,* the simultaneous oneness and difference of God and His energies. For example, when the sunshine is in your room, that does not mean the sun itself is in your room. The sun and its separated energies, like heat and light, are one in quality, but different in quantity.

DR. SINGH. But still, you say that one can see Kṛṣṇa in ordinary stone?

ŚRĪLA PRABHUPĀDA. Yes, why not? We see the stone as Kṛṣṇa's energy.

DR. SINGH. But can we worship Him within the stone?

ŚRĪLA PRABHUPĀDA. We can worship Him through His energy in the stone. But we cannot worship the stone *as* Kṛṣṇa. We cannot worship this bench *as* Kṛṣṇa. But we can worship everything because we see everything as Kṛṣṇa's energy. This tree is worshipable because both Kṛṣṇa and His energy are worshipable, but this does not mean we worship the tree in the same way as we worship the Deity of Kṛṣṇa in the temple.

In my childhood I was taught by my parents never to waste Kṛṣṇa's energy. They taught me that if even a small grain of rice was stuck between the floorboards, I should pick it up, touch it to my forehead and eat it to save it from being wasted. I was taught how to see everything in relation to Kṛṣṇa. That is Kṛṣṇa consciousness. We therefore do not like to see anything wasted or misused. We are teaching our disciples how to use everything for Kṛṣṇa and how to understand that everything is Kṛṣṇa. As Kṛṣṇa says in the *Bhagavad-gītā* [6.30]:

yo māṁ paśyati sarvatra
sarvaṁ ca mayi paśyati
tasyāhaṁ na praṇaśyāmi
sa ca me na praṇaśyati

"For one who sees Me everywhere and sees everything in Me, I am never lost, nor is he ever lost to Me."

The Eleventh Morning Walk

Recorded on May 15, 1973,
in Cheviot Hills Park, Los Angeles.

Śrīla Prabhupāda is accompanied by Dr. Singh and other students.

Detecting the Spirit Soul

DR. SINGH. Scientists find it very hard to see the spirit soul. They say its existence is very doubtful.

ŚRĪLA PRABHUPĀDA. How can they see it? It is too small to see. Who has that seeing power?

DR. SINGH. Still, they want to sense it by some means.

ŚRĪLA PRABHUPĀDA. If you inject someone with just one hundredth of a grain of very venomous poison, he dies immediately. No one can see the poison or how it acts, but it is acting nevertheless. So why don't the scientists see the soul by its action? In such cases we have to see by the effect. The *Vedas* say that because of the minute particle called the soul, the whole body is working nicely. If I pinch myself, I immediately feel it because I am conscious throughout the whole of my skin. But as soon as the soul is out of my body, which is the case when my body dies, you can take the same skin and cut and chop it, and nobody will protest. Why is this simple thing so hard to understand? Is this not detecting spirit?

DR. SINGH. We may detect the soul in this way, but what about God?

ŚRĪLA PRABHUPĀDA. First of all let us understand the soul. The soul is a sample God. If you can understand the sample, then you can understand the whole.

Modern Science: Help or Harm?

DR. SINGH. Scientists are in the process of trying to create life.

ŚRĪLA PRABHUPĀDA. "Process of"! "Trying to"! That we kick out; that we do not accept. A beggar is saying, "I am trying to be a millionaire." We say, "When you become a millionaire, then talk. Now you are a poor beggar; that is all." The scientists say they are trying, but suppose I ask you, "What are you?" Will you say, "I am trying to be . . ."? What are you now? That is the question. "We are trying" is not a proper answer, what to speak of a scientific proposition.

DR. SINGH. Well, although they haven't been able to create life so far, they say that soon they should be able to do so.

ŚRĪLA PRABHUPĀDA. Any rascal may say that. If you say, "In the future I shall be able to do something extraordinary," why should I trust or believe you?

DR. SINGH. Well, the scientists say they have done so much in the past and they will accomplish more in the future.

ŚRĪLA PRABHUPĀDA. In the past there was death, and people are dying now. So what have the scientists done?

DR. SINGH. Helped them.

ŚRĪLA PRABHUPĀDA. Scientists have helped to minimize the duration of life! Formerly men lived one hundred years; now they seldom live more than sixty or seventy years. And the scientists have discovered atomic energy; now they can kill millions of men. So they have helped only in dying. They have not helped in living, and still they dare to declare that they will create.

DR. SINGH. But now we have airplanes and—

ŚRĪLA PRABHUPĀDA. The scientists cannot stop death, they cannot stop birth, they cannot stop disease, and they cannot stop old age. So what have they done? Formerly people used to become old, and nowadays they are becoming old. Formerly people used to become diseased, and now they are becoming diseased. Now there is more medicine—and more disease. So what have they accomplished? Scientists have not helped improve the order of the world. We are going to challenge all the rascal scientists who say that life has grown out of matter. The fact is that matter has grown from life.

The Illusion of Progress

ŚRĪLA PRABHUPĀDA. How long can science cheat people? One hundred years, two hundred years? They cannot cheat them for all time.

DR. SINGH. Cheating has been going on since time immemorial, so perhaps they think they can continue forever.

ŚRĪLA PRABHUPĀDA. Not since time immemorial! Science has been cheating people for only the past two or three hundred years, not before that.

DR. SINGH. Oh, really?

ŚRĪLA PRABHUPĀDA. Yes, for the last two hundred years they have been preaching that life comes from matter—not for thousands of years. And the cheating will be finished in another fifty years.

DR. SINGH. Yes, now there is a so-called anti-intellectual movement. People are rebelling against science and modern progress.

ŚRĪLA PRABHUPĀDA. And what is that science? It is not science! It is ignorance. Ignorance is passing for science, and irreligion is passing for religion. But this cheating cannot go on for long, because some people are becoming intelligent.

DR. SINGH. In *Newsweek,* one of the largest magazines in the United States, there was an article about the degradation of Christianity. The article included a cartoon picturing the devil causing earthquakes. There was recently a very large earthquake in South America that killed many thousands of people. The cartoon attributed such things to the devil, and right next to him it showed Richard Nixon presenting himself as a follower of Christ but bombing Southeast Asia. In this cartoon, the devil turned to Richard Nixon and said, "It's hell keeping up with Christians."

ŚRĪLA PRABHUPĀDA. Yes, people will criticize in that way. People are becoming advanced. How long can they be cheated by so-called science and so-called religion? If Mr. Nixon loves his countrymen, why does he not love his country's cows? They are also born in the same land, and they have the same right to live. Why are they killed? "Thou shalt not kill." But the animals are being killed. That is imperfection. Kṛṣṇa embraces both the cows and Rādhārāṇī.[18] *That* is perfection. Kṛṣṇa even talks with the birds. One day on the bank of the Yamunā River, He was talking with a bird, because He speaks even in the languages of the birds. An old lady saw this and was struck with wonder: "Oh, He is talking with a bird!"

DR. SINGH. You mean He was actually talking the way the birds talk?

ŚRĪLA PRABHUPĀDA. Yes. One of Kṛṣṇa's qualities described in the *Vedas* is that He can speak any language. He is the father of all living beings, and the father can understand the language of his children.

Kṛṣṇa is the supreme enjoyer. Actually, except for those who are Kṛṣṇa conscious, no one can have any real knowledge, nor can anyone enjoy. One simply suffers, but he thinks the suffering is enjoyment. This is called *māyā,* or illusion. In America people work hard day and night, and they think, "I am enjoying." This is *māyā.* A conditioned soul cannot enjoy anything; he simply suffers, but he thinks he is enjoying.

Therefore, in *Śrīmad-Bhāgavatam* the conditioned soul is likened to the camel. The camel is very fond of eating thorny twigs that cut his tongue. While he is eating them, blood issues from his tongue and mixes with the thorny twigs. They become a little tasty, and he is thinking, "Oh, these twigs are very nice." That is called *māyā. Māyā* means "that which is not." *Mā* means "not," and *yā* means "this." So *māyā* means "not this." That is the explanation of *māyā,* or illusion. The scientists are in *māyā* because they think they are improving things and becoming happy. But this world, along with everything in it, will eventually be finished because it is *māyā;* it is not what we think it is. As *Śrīmad-Bhāgavatam* explains, the materialists are thinking they are becoming victorious, but they are actually being defeated.

The Twelfth Morning Walk

Recorded on May 17, 1973,
a misty morning, in Cheviot Hills Park, Los Angeles.

Śrīla Prabhupāda is accompanied by Dr. Singh, Karandhara dāsa adhikārī, Kṛṣṇakānti dāsa adhikārī and other students.

Yogic Weapons

ŚRĪLA PRABHUPĀDA. You have no power to drive away this mist. Scientists merely explain it with some word jugglery, saying that it contains certain chemicals. [He laughs.] But they have no power to drive it away.

DR. SINGH. They do have an explanation as to how the mist is formed.

ŚRĪLA PRABHUPĀDA. That they may have, and I may have that also, but that is not a very great credit. If you really know how it is formed, then you should be able to counteract it.

DR. SINGH. We know how it is formed.

ŚRĪLA PRABHUPĀDA. Then discover how to counteract it. Formerly, in Vedic warfare, the atomic *brahmāstra*[19] was used. And to counteract it, the opposing army would have to use a weapon that would transform it into water. But where is such a science today?

DR. SINGH. Mist is something like milk. Milk looks white, but actually it is a colloidal suspension of certain protein molecules. Similarly, fog is a colloidal suspension of water.

ŚRĪLA PRABHUPĀDA. So if you could create some type of fire, the mist would be immediately driven away; water can be driven away by fire. But that you cannot do. If you were to explode a bomb, it would generate heat, and all the mist would go away.

KARANDHARA. That might damage the whole city.

ŚRĪLA PRABHUPĀDA. Everyone knows that fire can counteract water, but you cannot drive away the mist without killing people or destroying property. But by nature's way, as soon as the sun rises, the mist is vanquished. The power of the sun is greater than your power. Therefore, you have to accept that inconceivable power exists.

Symptoms of God

ŚRĪLA PRABHUPĀDA. Without accepting the principle of inconceivable power, no one can understand God. God is not so cheap that any so-called *yogī* can become God. Such imitation gods are for rascals and fools. Those who are intelligent will test whether or not such a person has inconceivable power. We accept Kṛṣṇa as God because He has demonstrated His inconceivable power. As a child, Kṛṣṇa lifted a big hill. And Lord Rāma, an incarnation of Kṛṣṇa, constructed a bridge without pillars by floating stones on water. So one should not accept God cheaply. Nowadays, some rascal comes along and says, "I am an incarnation of God," and another rascal accepts him. But Lord Rāma and Lord Kṛṣṇa actually demonstrated Their inconceivable power. Sometimes people say the descriptions of Their activities are just stories or myths. But these literatures were composed by Vālmīki,[20] Vyāsadeva and other *ācāryas,* who are all great and vastly learned sages. Why would these great sages simply waste their time writing mythology? They never said it was mythology. They treated the accounts as actual facts. For instance, in the Tenth Canto of *Śrīmad-Bhāgavatam,* Vyāsadeva tells of a forest fire in Vṛndāvana. All of Kṛṣṇa's cowherd boyfriends became disturbed and looked to Kṛṣṇa for help. He simply swallowed up the whole fire. That is inconceivable mystic power. That is God. Because we are tiny samples of God, or Kṛṣṇa, we also possess inconceivable mystic power within our bodies—but only in very minute quantities.

Scientific Knowledge Comes From Kṛṣṇa

KṚṢṆAKĀNTI. The doctors marvel at the complex nature of the human brain.

ŚRĪLA PRABHUPĀDA. Yes, but it is not the brain that works the body; it is the spirit soul. Does a computer work by itself? No, a man works it. He pushes the button; *then* something happens.

Otherwise, what is the value of the machine? You can keep the machine for thousands of years, but it will not work until a man comes to push the button. But who is working, the machine or the man? Similarly, the human brain is also a machine, and it is working under the direction of Paramātmā, an expansion of God within everyone's heart.

Scientists should accept God and His mystic power. If they don't, they should be considered foolish. On the basis of transcendental knowledge, we are directly challenging many big scientists and philosophers. The other day, you brought that chemist, and I told him, "You are foolish." But he was not angry. He admitted it, and I defeated all his arguments. Perhaps you remember.

DR. SINGH. Yes. In fact, he acknowledged that perhaps Kṛṣṇa didn't give him all the procedural steps needed to perform his experiments.

ŚRĪLA PRABHUPĀDA. He is against Kṛṣṇa, so why should Kṛṣṇa give him any facilities? If you are against Kṛṣṇa and you want credit without Kṛṣṇa, you will fail. You must first be submissive, and then Kṛṣṇa will give you all facilities. We dare to face any scientist or philosopher and challenge him. How? On the strength of Kṛṣṇa. I know that when I talk with them, Kṛṣṇa will give me the necessary intelligence to defeat them. Otherwise, from the viewpoint of scientific qualification, they are much more qualified than we. We are laymen before them. But we know Kṛṣṇa, and Kṛṣṇa knows everything. Therefore we can challenge any scientists, just as a small child can challenge a very big man because he knows, "My father is here." He clutches the hand of his father, who makes sure that nobody can harm him.

DR. SINGH. Is the human form of life spoiled for those who do not try to understand Kṛṣṇa consciousness?

ŚRĪLA PRABHUPĀDA. Yes. People who do not try to understand their relationship with God simply die like animals—like cats and dogs. They take birth, eat, sleep, beget children and die. This is the sum total of their human lives. These rascals think, "I am this body." They have no information of *ātmā*. *Ātmā* means the self, or the individual soul. *Śrīmad-Bhāgavatam* and

Bhagavad-gītā give us knowledge about the *ātmā*, but people are unaware of this.

People are unaware of the knowledge given to human society in the Vedic literature. For example, the *Vedas* inform us that cow dung is pure. Here in America especially, people bring their dogs onto the street to pass stool. Of course, dog stool is very impure—germs thrive in it. But people are such rascals that they do not consider this; instead, they distribute dog stool everywhere. But there's no cow dung to be seen, even though the *Vedas* say that cow dung is pure. Here is a sign: "Littering Illegal." But dog stool is allowed. Just see how foolish people are. It is illegal to drop a paper on the grass, but your dog is allowed to pass stool. The government authorities will not allow you to bring even one mango from another country; but they will allow your dog to distribute its stool everywhere, although this stool is full of infectious germs.

The Space Program: A Childish Waste of Time and Money

DR. SINGH. When the astronauts returned from the moon to the surface of the earth, the scientists in the space program were very careful. They thought the astronauts might have brought some new germs as yet unknown, so they put the astronauts in quarantine for several days to make sure that—

ŚRĪLA PRABHUPĀDA. First of all, find out whether they have gone to the moon. I am not so sure. Sixteen years ago, when I wrote *Easy Journey to Other Planets,* I remarked that the scientists were childish in their attempts to explore outer space and would never be successful. Many years later, when I visited San Francisco, a press reporter asked me, "What is your opinion about the moon expedition?" I told him, "It is simply a waste of time and money, that's all."

KṚṢṆAKĀNTI. The space program recently had another failure.

ŚRĪLA PRABHUPĀDA. That is always happening. What was it?

KṚṢṆAKĀNTI. They sent up a space vehicle to orbit the earth and act as sort of a space outpost, but it failed. It cost two billion dollars.

ŚRĪLA PRABHUPĀDA. Why are they wasting time and money in that way?

KṚṢṆAKĀNTI. They were criticized in the newspapers.

ŚRĪLA PRABHUPĀDA. They are simply childish fools. What have they gained in the last—how many years? For how many years have they been trying to go to the moon?

DR. SINGH. It has been more than ten years. Russia started in 1957 with their sputnik.

ŚRĪLA PRABHUPĀDA. But they were trying for many years before that. So let us say that for twenty-five years they have been trying. They have not gained anything except dust, but still they are trying. How obstinate! The space program will never be successful.

DR. SINGH. They say that in the future they want to go to the subsurface of Mars.

ŚRĪLA PRABHUPĀDA. They are all becoming "big men" with their statements about the future.

DR. SINGH. They say that it will happen in about ten years.

ŚRĪLA PRABHUPĀDA. So what if they say one year? They may say ten years or one year, but we do not accept such propositions. We want to see what they are doing *now*.

DR. SINGH. They are developing their technology by using small-scale models.

ŚRĪLA PRABHUPĀDA. They are simply childish. In my childhood I used to watch the tramcars go along the rail. Once I thought, "I shall take a stick and touch it to the wire, and I shall also go along the rails." The scientists, with all their plans, are just as childish. They spend so much time and money, but what is their purpose? Their effort is hopeless because they do not actually know the purpose of life. The scientists are spending large sums of money, and politicians are financing them, but the result is zero. They are like a doctor who doesn't understand a particular disease, but who still says to his patient, "All right, first try this pill, and if that doesn't work, then try this pill." The doctor will never admit that he doesn't know the remedy for the disease. The scientists are simply bluffing and cheating. They cannot solve the real problems of life—birth, death, old age and disease—and therefore all their programs are taking place on the utopian platform, which in Sanskrit is called *ākāśa-puṣpa*. *Ākāśa-puṣpa* means "a flower from the sky." All their efforts to know the truth by exploring outer space are like trying to pluck a flower from the sky.

To give another example, the scientists act like foolish ducks. In India we may sometimes observe a duck following all day behind a bull. The duck is thinking that the testicles of the bull are a fish. In India this is a common sight. The bull is walking, and all day the duck is walking behind, following that big fish and thinking, "It will drop, and I will eat it."

The Thirteenth Morning Walk

Recorded on December 2, 1973,
on the shores of the Pacific Ocean near Los Angeles.

Śrīla Prabhupāda is accompanied by Dr. Singh, Hṛdayānanda dāsa Goswami, Kṛṣṇakāntī dāsa adhikārī and other students.

The Devotee Beyond Desires

ŚRĪLA PRABHUPĀDA. Now, who knows the difference between the *karmī,* the *jñānī,* the *yogī* and the *bhakta*?

HṚDAYĀNANDA DĀSA GOSWAMI: The *karmī* wants to enjoy the gross senses, the *jñānī* wants to enjoy the subtle mind—to mentally speculate—and the *yogī* wants to manipulate the universe with mystic powers.

ŚRĪLA PRABHUPĀDA. These are all material powers.

HṚDAYĀNANDA DĀSA GOSWAMI: And the *bhakta* has no material desires.

ŚRĪLA PRABHUPĀDA. Yes. And unless one is actually desireless, he cannot be happy. The *karmī,* the *jñānī* and the *yogī* are all full of desires; therefore they are unhappy. *Karmīs* are the most unhappy, the *jñānī* is a little less unhappy, and the *yogī* is still more advanced. But the *bhakta,* the devotee, is perfectly happy. Some *yogīs* have a mystic power that enables them to snatch pomegranates from trees in another country, thousands of miles away. Others can fly without an airplane. And some *yogīs* can hypnotize anyone. Then they point to someone and say, "This is God," and their victims believe them. I have actually seen such magical nonsense.

KṚṢṆAKĀNTI. Is the pure devotee more merciful than Kṛṣṇa?

ŚRĪLA PRABHUPĀDA. Yes. A real Vaiṣṇava, a real devotee, is even more merciful than Kṛṣṇa. Take Lord Jesus Christ, for example. It is said that Lord Jesus took everyone's sins upon himself, yet he was crucified. We can see how merciful he was. Today, rascals think, "Let us go on committing sinful activities; Christ has taken a contract to suffer for us." [There is a long, thoughtful silence.]

The Difference Between Matter and Spirit

DR. SINGH. Scientists say that trees also have consciousness.

ŚRĪLA PRABHUPĀDA. Yes, that is true, but a tree's consciousness and my consciousness are different. My consciousness is more developed. If you pinch my body, I will immediately protest. But if you cut a tree, it will not protest. Actually, everything has consciousness in it; it is simply a question of degree. The more covered consciousness is by matter, the more it is considered material. And the more consciousness is developed, the more it is considered spiritual. This is the difference between matter and spirit.

Spirit souls are everywhere. They are trying to come out of the earth. [Points to the grass.] As soon as there is an opportunity, they want to express their consciousness. Those souls who descend from higher planets to this planet sometimes fall down to the ground in raindrops. Then they become grass and gradually evolve to higher forms of life.

DR. SINGH. Oh, that is terrible.

ŚRĪLA PRABHUPĀDA. These are the workings of subtle energy. What do the scientists know about this? Actually, their knowledge is carried away by *māyā,* illusion, and they are thinking, "Oh, I am a very learned scholar."

Soul Transplants?

DR. SINGH. Śrīla Prabhupāda, what about heart transplants? We know that the spirit soul is within the heart. But nowadays doctors can replace an old heart with a new one. What happens to the spirit soul in each heart? Does the person who receives a new heart also get a new personality?

ŚRĪLA PRABHUPĀDA. No.

DR. SINGH. Why not?

ŚRĪLA PRABHUPĀDA. Suppose I get up from one chair and go sit in another chair. Does my personality change? I may change my seat, but does that mean I have changed?

DR. SINGH. But the heart is changed, and the heart contains the spirit soul.

ŚRĪLA PRABHUPĀDA. The *Vedas* describe the heart as a sitting place for the soul. So when they transplant hearts, they simply change the soul's seat. The same soul remains. If they could prove that by changing the heart they have increased the patient's duration of life, then that would prove they've caught the spirit soul. But they cannot increase the duration of life, because people have acquired their bodies by a superior arrangement. You have this body, and you must live within it for a certain period. If you simply change one of the parts of your body, that will not help you prolong your life. That is impossible. The doctors think that by changing the heart they will increase the duration of life, but that is not possible.

DR. SINGH. So a heart transplant is a kind of artificial transmigration of the soul from an old heart to a new one?

ŚRĪLA PRABHUPĀDA. Yes, it is something like that. Kṛṣṇa explains in the *Bhagavad-gītā* [2.13]:

dehino 'smin yathā dehe
kaumāraṁ yauvanaṁ jarā
tathā dehāntara-prāptir
dhīras tatra na muhyati

"As the embodied soul continually passes, in this body, from boyhood to youth to old age, the soul similarly passes into another body at death. The self-realized soul is not bewildered by such a change." Changing hearts is just a change of material bodily organs. The heart is not the real source of life, and therefore changing the heart does not prolong the duration of life.

DR. SINGH. Yes, most heart transplant patients live only a very short time after the operation. But is it ever possible to transplant the soul from one body to another?

ŚRĪLA PRABHUPĀDA. Sometimes certain *yogīs* can do that. They can find a better body and transfer themselves into it.

DR. SINGH. When the doctors perform a heart transplant, they take a heart from someone who has just died and exchange it for a weak heart in someone else's body. Does the soul from the dead heart change places with the soul in the weak living heart?

ŚRĪLA PRABHUPĀDA. No. The soul has already left the dead heart. There is no question of bringing in another soul.

DR. SINGH. Let me see if I understand you correctly. When the doctors remove the heart of a man who has just died, the soul has already left his heart. Then, when they transplant his dead heart into the body of the patient, the patient's soul passes into the transplanted heart.

ŚRĪLA PRABHUPĀDA. Yes. The soul is destined to live in a particular body for a certain number of years. You may change whatever part of the body you like, but you cannot change the duration of the life of that body.

DR. SINGH. So the heart is just a machine—an instrument?

ŚRĪLA PRABHUPĀDA. Yes. It is the sitting place of the soul.

A Mustard Seed in a Bag of Mustard Seeds

DR. SINGH. Śrīla Prabhupāda, biologists tell us that there are many species of life that can reproduce without sex. Do the *Vedas* agree with this?

ŚRĪLA PRABHUPĀDA. Oh, yes.

DR. SINGH. So we cannot curtail their reproduction?

ŚRĪLA PRABHUPĀDA. No. How could we? There are so many living entities that have come into this material world to enjoy life, and therefore reproduction must continue. This material world is like a jail. You cannot put an end to jails. As soon as one man leaves the jail, another is ready to enter it. This same question was discussed by Lord Caitanya Mahāprabhu.[21] One of His devotees, Vāsudeva Datta, said, "Please take all the living entities of this entire universe and release them from material bondage. And if You think they are too sinful to be rectified, then just give all their sins to me." But Caitanya Mahāprabhu said, "Suppose I were to take this entire universe and all the living entities with it. This is only one of innumerable universes. It is just like a mustard seed in a huge bag of mustard seeds. If you removed one seed from the bag, what would be the difference?" So reproduction cannot actually be stopped. Living entities are unlimited in number, and therefore it must continue.

DR. SINGH. You have said that this material world is like a correction house to teach one to get out of material entanglement and the cycle of repeated birth and death.

ŚRĪLA PRABHUPĀDA. Yes. Therefore you must practice Kṛṣṇa consciousness.

The Fourteenth Morning Walk

Recorded on December 3, 1973,
on the shores of the Pacific Ocean near Los Angeles.

Śrīla Prabhupāda is accompanied by Dr. Singh, Dr. W. H. Wolf-Rottkay and other students.

The Origin of the Interplanetary Gases

DR. SINGH. The scientists say that at one point the earth was composed of dust particles floating in some gaseous material. Then, in due course, this colloidal suspension condensed and formed the earth.

ŚRĪLA PRABHUPĀDA. That may be, but where did the gas come from?

DR. SINGH. They say it just existed!

ŚRĪLA PRABHUPĀDA. Kṛṣṇa says in *Bhagavad-gītā* [7.4]:

bhūmir āpo 'nalo vāyuḥ
khaṁ mano buddhir eva ca
ahaṅkāra itīyaṁ me
bhinnā prakṛtir aṣṭadhā

"Earth, water, fire, air, ether, mind, intelligence and false ego—all together these eight comprise My separated material energies." Here Kṛṣṇa explains that *vāyu* (gas) came from Him. And finer than *vāyu* is *kham* (ether), finer than ether is mind, finer than mind is intelligence, finer than intelligence is false ego, and finer than false ego is the soul. But the scientists do not know this. They understand only gross things. They mention gas, but where does the gas come from?

DR. SINGH. That they cannot answer.

ŚRĪLA PRABHUPĀDA. But *we* can answer. From *Śrīmad-Bhāgavatam* we know that gas has come from *kham,* or ether,

ether comes from mind, mind comes from intelligence, intelligence comes from false ego, and false ego comes from the soul.

DR. SINGH. The scientists argue that before Darwin's biophysical type of evolution could take place, there had to be what they call prebiotic chemistry, or chemical evolution.

ŚRĪLA PRABHUPĀDA. Yes. And the term "chemical evolution" means that chemicals have an origin, and that origin is spirit, or life. A lemon produces citric acid, and our bodies produce many chemicals in urine, blood, and bodily secretions. This is proof that life produces chemicals, not that chemicals produce life.

DR. SINGH. Scientists say that once the seed of life is present in the cells, then the living entity automatically develops and functions.

ŚRĪLA PRABHUPĀDA. Yes, but who gives the seed? In the *Bhagavad-gītā* [7.10] Kṛṣṇa answers this question. *Bījaṁ māṁ sarva-bhūtānāṁ viddhi pārtha sanātanam:* "O son of Pṛthā, know that I am the original seed of all existences." And later [14.4]:

sarva-yoniṣu kaunteya
mūrtayaḥ sambhavanti yāḥ
tāsāṁ brahma mahad yonir
ahaṁ bīja-pradaḥ pitā

"It should be understood that all species of life, O son of Kuntī, are made possible by birth in this material nature, and that I am the seed-giving father."

Giving Credit to the Primal Creator

DR. WOLF-ROTTKAY. But in all humility, Śrīla Prabhupāda, suppose the scientists actually succeed in artificially creating a living cell. What would you say?

ŚRĪLA PRABHUPĀDA. What would be their credit? They would only be imitating what already exists in nature. People are very fond of imitations. If a man in a nightclub imitates a dog, people will go and pay money to watch him. But when they see a real dog barking, they don't pay any attention to it.

DR. SINGH. Śrīla Prabhupāda, the idea of chemical evolution came from a Russian biologist in 1920. He demonstrated that before biochemical evolution, the earth's atmosphere was in a state of reduction. In other words, it was mostly full of hydrogen, with very little oxygen. Then, in due course, the sun's radiation caused these hydrogen molecules to form into different chemicals.

ŚRĪLA PRABHUPĀDA. This is a side study. First of all, where did the hydrogen come from? The scientists simply study the middle of the process; they do not study the origin. We must know the beginning. There is an airplane. [Indicates an airplane appearing on the horizon.] Would you say the origin of that machine is the sea? A foolish person might say that all of a sudden a light appeared in the sea, and that's how the airplane was created. But is that a scientific explanation? The scientists' explanations are similar. They say, "This existed, and then all of a sudden, by chance, that occurred." This is not science. Science means to explain the original cause.

Perhaps the scientists can create imitations of nature, but why should we give them credit? We should give credit to the original creator, God; that is our philosophy.

DR. SINGH. When a scientist discovers some natural law, he usually names it after himself.

ŚRĪLA PRABHUPĀDA. Yes, exactly. The law is already there in nature, but the rascal wants to take credit for it.

Gerontology: Prolonging the Suffering

DR. SINGH. They are actually fighting against the laws of nature, but often they take pleasure in the struggle.

ŚRĪLA PRABHUPĀDA. That pleasure is childish. Suppose a child builds a sand castle on the beach with great effort. He may take pleasure in it, but that is childish pleasure. That is not a grown man's pleasure. Materialistic men have created a standard of false happiness. They have created a gorgeous arrangement for a comfortable civilization, but it is all false because they cannot create a situation in which they will be able to enjoy it. At any moment, anyone can be kicked out by death, and all his enjoyment will be finished.

DR. SINGH. That is why they say that God hasn't given us everything—because we are not able to live here forever.

ŚRĪLA PRABHUPĀDA. But God has given them everything necessary to live peacefully, and everything necessary to understand Him. So why will they not inquire about God? Instead, they do things that help them forget God.

DR. SINGH. Now the scientists have organized a whole department in science called gerontology, in which they study how to prolong life.

ŚRĪLA PRABHUPĀDA. Their real aim should be to stop the suffering. Suppose an old man is in great pain, suffering from many diseases, and suddenly the doctors increase his life-span. What is the profit?

DR. SINGH. That is what they do with heart transplants.

ŚRĪLA PRABHUPĀDA. It is nonsense! Let them stop death; *that* would be an achievement. Let them stop all disease; ah, *that* would be an achievement. They cannot do these things! Therefore, I say that all their research is simply a struggle for existence. Kṛṣṇa says in *Bhagavad-gītā* [15.7]:

mamaivāṁśo jīva-loke
jīva-bhūtaḥ sanātanaḥ
manaḥ-ṣaṣṭhānīndriyāṇi
prakṛti-sthāni karṣati

"The living entities in this conditioned world are My eternal, fragmental parts. Due to conditioned life, they are struggling very hard with the six senses, which include the mind."

STUDENT. Now there is a shortage of oil.

ŚRĪLA PRABHUPĀDA. Yes, we have built a civilization that is dependent on oil. This is against nature's law, and therefore there is now an oil shortage. By nature's law, winter is now coming. Scientists cannot stop it and turn it into summer. They wrongly think they are in control of nature. In *Bhagavad-gītā* Kṛṣṇa informs us that the living being thinks himself to be the doer of activities that are in actuality carried out by nature. The sun is now rising. Can they make it dark? And when it is dark, can they command the sun, "Get up!"

They do not realize that if they really want to conquer nature, they should try to conquer birth, death, old age and disease. In *Bhagavad-gītā* [7.14] Kṛṣṇa says:

daivī hy eṣā guṇamayī
mama māyā duratyayā
mām eva ye prapadyante
māyām etāṁ taranti te

"This divine energy of Mine, consisting of the three modes of material nature, is difficult to overcome. But those who have surrendered unto Me can easily cross beyond it."

DR. SINGH. So, is it very hard to overcome nature's laws?

ŚRĪLA PRABHUPĀDA. For the materialists, it is impossible. But if one surrenders to Kṛṣṇa, it becomes easy.

The Real Origin of Species

DR. SINGH. To explain why there are so many varieties of living entities, the scientists say that at a certain time during evolution, the cells' genes, which normally reproduce themselves perfectly for the next generation, sometimes make a mistake in copying—something like the printing press that sometimes makes mistakes. In some circumstances these mistakes, or mutations, have stood, and different species of living entities have been formed because of the difference in the genes.

ŚRĪLA PRABHUPĀDA. But that "mistake" has been continuing since time immemorial, for you will find that all varieties of living entities have always existed. Therefore the "mistake" is eternal. But when a "mistake" is permanent, it is not a mistake; it is intelligence!

DR. SINGH. But scientists say that if there were no mutations, then there would be only one kind of living entity in the whole universe.

ŚRĪLA PRABHUPĀDA. No. Every living entity has a different mind, and therefore there are so many different species of life to accommodate the different mentalities. For example, we are walking here, but most people are not coming to join us, because they have different mentalities than we do. Why does this difference exist?

DR. SINGH. Maybe it is a mistake.

ŚRĪLA PRABHUPĀDA. It is not a mistake. It is their desire, and at the time of death everyone will get a body exactly according to his desire. Kṛṣṇa says in *Bhagavad-gītā* [8.6]:

yaṁ yaṁ vāpi smaran bhāvaṁ
tyajaty ante kalevaram
taṁ tam evaiti kaunteya
sadā tad-bhāva-bhāvitaḥ

"Whatever state of being one remembers when he quits his body, that state he will attain without fail." What you are thinking of at the time of death exactly determines your next body. Nature will give you the body; the decision is not in your hands, but in nature's, and she is working under the direction of God.

DR. SINGH. But science seems to have evidence that different species of life do arise by mistakes.

ŚRĪLA PRABHUPĀDA. That is *their* mistake! In the laws of nature there are no mistakes. In railway cars there are first-class, second-class and third-class sections. If you purchase a third-class ticket but by mistake go to the first-class section, you will not be allowed to stay there. It is not a mistake that there are sections; that is the arrangement. But it is your mistake that you have gone to the wrong section. So, God is so thorough that He knows all the mistakes that will be made. Therefore, according to the mistakes you commit, you enter a particular body: "Here, come here. The body is ready." There are 8,400,000 species of life, and nature works, assigning different bodies, with mathematical precision. When the government builds a city, it builds a prison even before the city is completed, because the government knows that there will be many criminals who will have to go to prison. This is not the government's mistake; it is the mistake of the criminals. Because they become criminals, they have to go there. It is *their* mistake.

In nature there are no mistakes. Kṛṣṇa says:

mayādhyakṣeṇa prakṛtiḥ
sūyate sacarācaram

hetunānena kaunteya
jagad viparivartate

"This material nature is working under My direction, O son of Kuntī, and producing all moving and nonmoving beings." [Bg. 9.10] Nature works under the supervision of God, Kṛṣṇa, so how can nature make mistakes? But *we* commit mistakes, we are illusioned, our senses are imperfect, and we cheat. That is the difference between God and man. God does not have imperfect senses; His senses are perfect.

Satisfied Animals

DR. WOLF-ROTTKAY. Because our senses are defective, the technological enlargements of our senses must also be defective, of course.

DR. SINGH. The microscopes with which we detect things must also be defective.

ŚRĪLA PRABHUPĀDA. Material existence *means* defective existence. If you construct something with defective knowledge and imperfect senses, whatever you construct must be defective.

DR. SINGH. Even if scientists devised a perfect microscope, they would still have to look through it with defective eyes.

ŚRĪLA PRABHUPĀDA. Yes. That is right. Therefore we conclude that whatever the scientists may say is defective.

DR. SINGH. But they seem quite satisfied.

ŚRĪLA PRABHUPĀDA. The ass is also satisfied. The ass is satisfied to carry the load of the washerman. Everyone is satisfied, even the worm in the stool. That is nature's law.

DR. WOLF-ROTTKAY. It is said that even the pauper is proud of his penny.

ŚRĪLA PRABHUPĀDA. Yes. In some parts of India one may sometimes see a dog starving to death. But as soon as it gets a female dog, it is satisfied with having sex. Is that satisfaction? The dog is starving, but still it is satisfied with sex.

The Fifteenth Morning Walk

Recorded on December 7, 1973,
on the shores of the Pacific Ocean near Los Angeles.

Śrīla Prabhupāda is accompanied by Dr. Singh, Dr. W. H. Wolf-Rottkay and another student.

Getting the Eyes to See God

STUDENT. For the last one hundred fifty years, one of the major problems of Western theologians has been the relationship between reason and faith. They have been seeking to understand faith through reason, but they have been unable to find the relationship between the reasoning abilities and faith. Some of them have *faith* in God, but their *reason* tells them there is no God. For instance, they would say that when we offer *prasāda* to the Lord, it is only faith to think that He accepts it, because we cannot see Him.

ŚRĪLA PRABHUPĀDA. *They* cannot see Him, but *I* can see Him. I see God, and therefore I offer *prasāda* to Him. Because they cannot see Him, they must come to me so I can open their eyes. They are blind—suffering from cataracts—so I shall operate, and they will see. That is our program.

STUDENT. Scientists say that their common ground of objectivity is what they can perceive with their senses.

ŚRĪLA PRABHUPĀDA. Yes, they can perceive things with their senses, but very imperfectly. They perceive the sand with their senses, but can they see who has made the sand? Here is the sand, and here is the sea; they can be seen by direct perception. But how can one directly perceive the *origin* of the sand and the sea?

STUDENT. The scientists say that if the sand and the sea were made by God, we would be able to see Him, just as we can see the sand and the sea themselves.

ŚRĪLA PRABHUPĀDA. Yes, they can see God, but they must get the eyes to see Him. They are blind. Therefore they must first come to me for treatment. The *śāstras* say that one must go to a *guru* to be treated so that one can understand God. How can they see God with blind eyes?

STUDENT. But seeing God is supramundane. Scientists only consider mundane vision.

ŚRĪLA PRABHUPĀDA. Everything is supramundane. For instance, you may think there is nothing in the clear sky—that it is vacant—but your eyes are deficient. In the sky there are innumerable planets you cannot see because your eyes are limited. Therefore, because it is not in your power to perceive, you have to accept my word: "Yes, there are millions of stars out there." Is space vacant because you cannot see the stars? No. Only the deficiency of your senses leads you to think so.

STUDENT. The scientists will admit their ignorance of some things, but they say they cannot accept what they cannot see.

ŚRĪLA PRABHUPĀDA. If they're ignorant, they have to accept knowledge from someone who knows the truth.

STUDENT. But they say, "What if what we are told is wrong?"

ŚRĪLA PRABHUPĀDA. Then that is their misfortune. Because their imperfect senses cannot perceive God, they have to hear it from an authority. That is the process. If they don't approach the authority—if they approach a cheater—that is their misfortune. But the process is that wherever your senses cannot act, you must approach an authority to learn the facts.

The Frustration of the Atheists

DR. SINGH. The difficulty is that in a group of atheists, you can't prove the existence of God.

ŚRĪLA PRABHUPĀDA. The atheists are rascals. Let us teach the others—those who are reasonable. Everything has been made by someone: the sand has been made by someone, the water has been made by someone, and the sky has been made by someone. Kṛṣṇa consciousness means learning who that someone is.

DR. SINGH. The scientists will say, "Present that someone to me so I can see Him."

ŚRĪLA PRABHUPĀDA. And I answer them, "I am presenting that someone to you, but you have to take the training as well." You have to qualify your eyes to see that someone. If you are blind, but you do not want to go to the physician, how will you be cured of your blindness and see? You have to be treated; that is the injunction.

STUDENT. That step requires faith.

ŚRĪLA PRABHUPĀDA. Yes, but not blind faith—practical faith. If you want to learn anything, you must go to an expert. That is not blind faith; it is practical faith. You cannot learn anything by yourself.

STUDENT. If somebody is actually sincere, will he always meet a bona fide *guru*?

ŚRĪLA PRABHUPĀDA. Yes. *Guru-kṛṣṇa-prasāde pāya bhakti-latā-bīja.* Kṛṣṇa is within you, and as soon as He sees that you are sincere, He will send you to the right person.

STUDENT. And if you are not completely sincere, you will get a cheater for a teacher?

ŚRĪLA PRABHUPĀDA. Yes. If you want to be cheated, Kṛṣṇa will send you to a cheater. Kṛṣṇa is superintelligent. If you are a cheater, He will cheat you perfectly. But if you are actually sincere, then He will give you the right guidance. In *Bhagavad-gītā* [15.15] Kṛṣṇa says, *sarvasya cāhaṁ hṛdi sanniviṣṭo mattaḥ smṛtir jñānam apohanaṁ ca:* "I am seated in everyone's heart, and from Me come remembrance, knowledge and forgetfulness." Kṛṣṇa speaks of both remembrance and forgetfulness. If you are a cheater, Kṛṣṇa will give you the intelligence to forget Him forever.

STUDENT. But the atheists are in control. They have the dominance.

ŚRĪLA PRABHUPĀDA. One kick of *māyā* and all their dominance is finished in one second. That is the nature of *māyā*. The atheists are under control, but due to *māyā,* or illusion, they think they're free.

moghāśā mogha-karmāṇo
mogha-jñānā vicetasaḥ
rākṣasīṁ āsurīṁ caiva
prakṛtiṁ mohinīṁ śritāḥ

"Those who are bewildered are attracted by demoniac and atheistic views. In that deluded condition, their hopes for liberation, their fruitive activities and their culture of knowledge are all defeated." [Bg. 9.12] Because they are bewildered, all their hopes are frustrated. That is stated here in *Bhagavad-gītā,* and that is actually happening. So many of their big plans, like this moon project, are frustrated, but they still claim that they can dominate nature.

DR. SINGH. They do not want to come to their senses.

ŚRĪLA PRABHUPĀDA. Therefore they are rascals.

Scientists Bravely Going to Hell

ŚRĪLA PRABHUPĀDA. A sensible man will take a good lesson, but a rascal will never take a good lesson. There is a story of a great poet named Kalidāsa, who was a great rascal also. Once, Kalidāsa was sitting on the branch of a tree and simultaneously cutting it. A gentleman asked him, "Why are you cutting this tree limb? You will fall down."

Kalidāsa replied, "No, no, I will not fall down." So he kept cutting the limb, and he fell down. The conclusion is that he was a rascal because he would not take good advice. By their so-called scientific advancement, scientists are going to hell. But they do not listen when they are told; therefore they are rascals. Rascals repeatedly make a plan, see it frustrated, and again make another plan. This plan is also frustrated, so they make *another* plan. Yet when we try to explain to them that all their materialistic plans will be unsuccessful and useless, they refuse to listen. That is rascaldom. The rascals repeatedly chew the chewed. At home, in the street, at the nightclub, at the theater—wherever he is, sex in its different varieties is his only pleasure.

STUDENT. Śrīla Prabhupāda, one could say that that is bravery.

ŚRĪLA PRABHUPĀDA. Yes, you can *say* that, but that bravery is their rascaldom. They are bravely going to hell, that's all. Once, one man was chasing another man, and the man who was chasing asked, "Why are you fleeing? Are you afraid of me?"

The other man replied, "I am not afraid of you. Why should I *not* run? Why should I stop?"

In the same way, the gross materialist is bravely going to hell. "Why should I stop with my sinful activities?" he says. "I will bravely face any reaction."

DR. SINGH. They are crazy.

ŚRĪLA PRABHUPĀDA. Yes, crazy. The *Vedas* say that once a man becomes crazy, or haunted by ghosts, he speaks all kinds of nonsense. Similarly, anyone under the influence of the material energy is crazy. Therefore he talks only nonsense, that's all. Though scientists are not expert in science, they *are* expert in bluffing others and juggling words.

Mystic Television

DR. SINGH. They now have things they did not have before, like telephones, televisions, airplanes, missiles and many other new discoveries.

ŚRĪLA PRABHUPĀDA. But there are better telephones that they do not know about. In *Bhagavad-gītā,* Sañjaya demonstrated this when he was sitting with his master, Dhṛtarāṣṭra, and relating all the affairs that were taking place far away on the Battlefield of Kurukṣetra. Sañjaya's vision was actually greater than the telephone. It was mystic television. It was television within the heart, for he was sitting in a room far from the battlefield and still seeing everything that was occurring there. In *Bhagavad-gītā,* Dhṛtarāṣṭra inquired of Sañjaya, "How are my sons and nephews? What are they doing?" Then Sañjaya described how Duryodhana was going to Droṇācārya, what Droṇācārya was speaking, how Duryodhana was replying, and so on. Even though these activities were too far away to be seen by ordinary eyes, Sañjaya could see and describe them through his mystic power. That is real science.

DR. SINGH. Some scientists say that we have improved on nature by making things like plastic and medicine.

ŚRĪLA PRABHUPĀDA. In Vedic times people ate on silver and golden plates, but now the scientists have improved things with plastic plates. [Laughter.]

DR. SINGH. The plastic has become a great problem because they cannot get rid of it. There is no way to dispose of it. It just continues to pile up.

Here Is the Proof

DR. WOLF-ROTTKAY. The materialists would be more sincere if they said, "We don't want to be taken out of our dream. We want to continue trying to enjoy our senses with all our machines." But they will not admit that their attempts to enjoy always fail.

ŚRĪLA PRABHUPĀDA. That is their foolishness. Eventually they have to admit it.

DR. WOLF-ROTTKAY. But they say, "Try, try again."

ŚRĪLA PRABHUPĀDA. How can they try? Suppose you cannot see because you are suffering from cataracts. If you try to see—you try, try, try, try, try. Is that the cure for cataracts? No. You will never be cured like that. You must go to a physician, who will perform a surgical operation to restore your eyesight. You cannot see by trying and trying.

DR. WOLF-ROTTKAY. That is just what they do not want to accept—that all their efforts to know the truth by materialistic science have failed.

ŚRĪLA PRABHUPĀDA. They are foolish. They will not take good advice. If you give a rascal some good advice, he will become angry, just like a serpent. Suppose you bring a serpent into your home and say, "My dear serpent, please live with me. Every day I will give you nice food—milk and bananas." The snake will be very pleased, but the result will be that its poison will increase, and one day you will say, "Ah!" [Imitates a bitten person.]

DR. WOLF-ROTTKAY. But the scientists will never give up hope.

ŚRĪLA PRABHUPĀDA. Their plans are being frustrated at every moment, but still they are hoping.

STUDENT. Śrīla Prabhupāda, one librarian wanted me to prove that *Bhagavad-gītā* was five thousand years old. He wanted to see a copy that was written down five thousand years ago.

ŚRĪLA PRABHUPĀDA. Suppose I go into a dark room and say to the person inside, "The sun has risen. Come out!" The person in darkness may say, "Where is the proof that there is light? First prove it to me; then I will come out." I may plead with him, "Please, please, just come out and see." But if he does not come out to see, he remains ignorant, waiting for proof. So, if you simply read *Bhagavad-gītā* you will see everything. Come and see. Here is the proof.

The Sixteenth Morning Walk

Recorded on December 10, 1973,
on the shores of the Pacific Ocean near Los Angeles.

Śrīla Prabhupāda is accompanied by Dr. Singh, Hṛdayānanda dāsa Goswami and other students.

The Meaning of "Supreme"

ŚRĪLA PRABHUPĀDA. What is the meaning of supremacy in this material world? Why do you accept President Nixon as the supreme person within your state?

DR. SINGH. Because he has some power.

ŚRĪLA PRABHUPĀDA. Yes. And why is he supreme? Because as the government's number one servant, he gets the highest salary, has all the best facilities, and his order is final.

DR. SINGH. He has the power to convince others.

ŚRĪLA PRABHUPĀDA. No. You may not agree with him, but because he is supreme, you have to accept his order. That is his position. It does not depend on your acceptance or nonacceptance. That is the meaning of supremacy, is it not? The Vedic literature says that one who has the symptoms of supremacy is fortunate. The supremely fortunate person is God. *Lakṣmī-sahasra-śata-sambhrama-sevyamānam:* "He is served by hundreds and thousands of *lakṣmīs,* or goddesses of fortune." [*Brahma-saṁhitā* 5.29] Here on this planet we are begging a little favor from the goddess of fortune. But Kṛṣṇa is always worshiped by many thousands of goddesses of fortune.

DR. SINGH. To conceive of anyone so fortunate is beyond our thinking capacity.

ŚRĪLA PRABHUPĀDA. Yes. Therefore Kṛṣṇa is *acintya,* inconceivable. We cannot estimate how great or fortunate He is! *Acintya* means "that which we cannot estimate." We can see only a part of God's opulence—this material nature—which is only a partial exhibition of God's potencies. The Supreme Personality has many potencies. He has inferior energies and superior energies. In *Bhagavad-gītā* [7.4] Kṛṣṇa says:

bhūmir āpo 'nalo vāyuḥ
khaṁ mano buddhir eva ca
ahaṅkāra itīyaṁ me
bhinnā prakṛtir aṣṭadhā

"Earth, water, fire, air, ether, mind, intelligence and false ego—all together these eight comprise My separated material energies." In the next verse of *Bhagavad-gītā,* Kṛṣṇa describes His superior energy (*parā prakṛti*), which is manifested as the spiritual world. So, if in the inferior, material energy there are so many wonderful things, just imagine how much more important and how much more wonderful things are in the spiritual world. This is the meaning of *superior.*

The Mysteries of Yogic Power

HṚDAYĀNANDA DĀSA GOSWAMI. And are all the varieties of life we see on earth contained in the spiritual world?

ŚRĪLA PRABHUPĀDA. Yes. And, moreover, if in this inferior energy there are so many wonderful varieties of life, just think how wonderful are the superior varieties of life in the spiritual world. Even in this material universe, the inhabitants of some planets are far superior to those on other planets. For example, people on earth practice mystic *yoga* for achieving wonderful powers, but people on the planet called Siddhaloka have these great yogic powers naturally. On earth it is natural that a bird can fly; but we cannot, except with costly machines. However, on such planets as Siddhaloka, the residents can fly even from one planet to another without machines. They can go to other planets simply at will. Even on earth there are some *yogīs* who can take their bath early in the morning in four places at once—Jagannātha Purī, Rāmeśvara, Hardwar and Dvārakā.[22] One *yogī* friend used to visit my father in Calcutta. The *yogī* told him that when he (the *yogī*) would simply sit down and touch his *guru,* he would travel from Calcutta to Dvārakā in two minutes. That is yogic power. So what are today's airplanes? Durvāsā Muni traveled all over the universe and up to Vaikuṇṭha[23] within one year. According to modern calculations, certain planets in this universe are more than forty thousand light-years[24] distant from the earth. This means it would take forty thousand years to reach these planets if you traveled at the speed of light. Even if they had the means, how could the astronauts live for forty thousand years? So, why are they so proud?

DR. SINGH. The scientists have a theory that they can produce a machine that will travel at the speed of light.

ŚRĪLA PRABHUPĀDA. That is rascaldom. They say that, but they will never be able to do it.

Vedic Cosmology

ŚRĪLA PRABHUPĀDA. There are many invisible planets and stars. For example, when the Rāhu planet passes before the sun and moon, there is an eclipse. But the scientists describe an eclipse differently. Actually, the Rāhu planet causes an eclipse. There are many questionable points regarding the modern scientists' theory of the eclipse. Their explanation is incorrect according to Vedic information.

DR. SINGH. But the scientists say that they can prove their theories.

ŚRĪLA PRABHUPĀDA. They say that science proves everything. But that is nonsense. The scientist has proved everything except what he is. *That* he does not know. And why does he die? That also he does not know. That is the extent of his knowledge.

DR. SINGH. They can make a model of the universe. They can make a model of the planets and the moon.

ŚRĪLA PRABHUPĀDA. If they can make things, why don't they make an imitation sun to save electricity? These rascals say everything, but they cannot do anything. That is their position. If they can make a model of the universe, let them make a big model of the sun. Then in the dark night we will not have to spend so much money on electricity. But they cannot do it. Yet they speak big, big words, simply to take money from the taxpayers. They say they know the composition of the moon and the composition of the sun, so why can't they make them? Why can't they create an artificial sun so that the people of Iceland and Greenland can be saved from so much cold?

God Is Never Zero

ŚRĪLA PRABHUPĀDA. Lord Caitanya Mahāprabhu once gave the example of the jewel called *cintāmaṇi,* which produces many other jewels while remaining as it is.

oṁ pūrṇam adaḥ pūrṇam idaṁ
pūrṇāt pūrṇam udacyate
pūrṇasya pūrṇam ādāya
pūrṇam evāvaśiṣyate
[*Śrī Īśopaniṣad* Invocation]

The meaning of this verse is that although everything emanates from the Personality of Godhead, He never diminishes. Here on earth the petrol is running out, and this is becoming a terrible problem, but the sun is still shining and will continue to shine for an untold number of years. And Kṛṣṇa can create millions of suns; in fact, He has already done so. But He is still fully potent. He has lost nothing. That is God, and that is the supreme energy of God, *acintya-śakti.*

We have some money to spend, and the next day our account becomes zero. Rascals say that ultimate truth is zero, *śūnyavāda.* They do not know that God is never zero—that He is always positive. So we must have a clear idea of God. Theologians should take these ideas from Vedic descriptions and not be misled by fools and rascals. God and His full energies are explained in the Vedic literatures. Our energy is lost, but God's is not. That is the difference between God and us. I cannot walk swiftly or do so many other things that a young man can do, because I have lost my youthful energy. But God is always youthful. *Advaitam acyutam anādim ananta-rūpam ādyaṁ purāṇa-puruṣaṁ nava-yauvanaṁ ca:* "Kṛṣṇa, the Supreme Personality of Godhead, is absolute, infallible and beginningless. Expanded into unlimited forms, He is the original person, the oldest, and always appearing as a fresh youth." [*Brahma-saṁhitā* 5.33] Kṛṣṇa also says in *Bhagavad-gītā, īśvaraḥ sarva-*

bhūtānāṁ hṛd-deśe 'rjuna tiṣṭhati: "The Supreme Lord is situated in everyone's heart." He is also within every atom. But still He is one. That is God. And He is *advaita,* without duality. Not that He is living within your heart and a different personality is living within my heart. No, they are one. God is everywhere by His all-pervasive features, and He is also localized; yet He is still one.

The Absolute Nature of Kṛṣṇa's Love

DR. SINGH. In some Western theological literature, Śrīla Prabhupāda, they say that God is love.

ŚRĪLA PRABHUPĀDA. God is everything. Why do they say He is this or that? Anything is God because He is absolute. His love and His enmity are the same. In the material world, we distinguish between love and animosity. But God's animosity and God's love are the same thing. Therefore, He is called *acintya,* or inconceivable. God's love for the *gopīs*[25] and God's enmity for Kaṁsa[26] achieved the same result. Both Kaṁsa and the *gopīs* went to the spiritual world. Also, Pūtanā[27] came to poison Kṛṣṇa, and mother Yaśodā was always anxious to save Kṛṣṇa, the naughty child, lest He be harmed. So mother Yaśodā and Pūtanā are opposite, but they both achieved the same results. Kṛṣṇa thought, "I have sucked Pūtanā's breast, so now she is My mother. She must reach the same destination as Yaśodā." This is the absolute nature of Kṛṣṇa's enmity and Kṛṣṇa's love.

vadanti tat tattva-vidas
tattvaṁ yaj jñānaṁ advayam
brahmeti paramātmeti
bhagavān iti śabdyate

"Learned transcendentalists who know the Absolute Truth call this nondual substance Brahman, Paramātmā or Bhagavān." [*Śrīmad-Bhāgavatam* 1.2.11] God has His impersonal, all-pervasive feature (known as Brahman) and His localized Paramātmā feature. At the same time He is Bhagavān, which is His original, personal, transcendental form. The three are different but the same. This is the nature of God, *acintya-bhedābheda-tattva*—simultaneously one and different. One who has reached the personal conception of Bhagavān has automatically reached Brahman and Paramātmā. They are all Kṛṣṇa, but there is a difference between them. They are simultaneously one and different.

Accepting Knowledge From a Learned Person

DR. SINGH. Śrīla Prabhupāda, many people have difficulty accepting God.

ŚRĪLA PRABHUPĀDA. They are diseased, but they do not want to be treated. If they do not agree to be treated, that is their fault. One who is not Kṛṣṇa conscious—God conscious—is a madman. Under the power of the illusory energy—the inferior, material energy—he talks only nonsense, just like someone haunted by a ghost. You must approach a person who is learned. You must find such a person, a *guru,* and surrender to him. Then question him, and whatever answers you get from him you must accept. That is the process for understanding God. You must first find the *guru;* then you must satisfy him by service and by surrendering unto him. The *guru* will explain everything. Kṛṣṇa explains in *Bhagavad-gītā* [4.34]:

tad viddhi praṇipātena
paripraśnena sevayā
upadekṣyanti te jñānaṁ
jñāninas tattva-darśinaḥ

"Just try to learn the truth by approaching a spiritual master. Inquire from him submissively and render service unto him. The self-realized soul can impart knowledge unto you because he has seen the truth."

Appendixes

Notes

1. Vedic knowledge was originally handed down as one *Veda*. About five thousand years ago the sage Vyāsadeva divided it into four *Vedas* (*Ṛg, Yajur, Sāma* and *Atharva*) so that less intelligent people might understand it. Vyāsadeva was an empowered incarnation of God. He also undertook the task of expanding the *Vedas* into eighteen *Purāṇas* and the *Mahābhārata,* and he summed up all the Vedic literature in the *Vedānta-sūtra.* But he was still dissatisfied with this colossal literary achievement. Therefore, under the direction of his spiritual master, Nārada Muni, he wrote the *Śrīmad-Bhāgavatam,* which is "the ripened fruit of Vedic knowledge."

2. *Bhagavad-gītā* is widely renowned throughout the world as the essence of Vedic knowledge. It contains the sacred instructions given by Lord Kṛṣṇa, the Supreme Personality of Godhead, to Arjuna, His intimate devotee, on the Battlefield of Kurukṣetra. In these instructions Lord Kṛṣṇa gives a scientific exposition of the perfect path to self-realization in the present dark age of hypocrisy and quarrel.

Originally written in Sanskrit, *Bhagavad-gītā* has been published in almost every language in the world (there are more than six hundred English translations alone), but *Bhagavad-gītā As It Is,* by His Divine Grace A.C. Bhaktivedanta Swami Prabhupāda, is the first English translation and commentary by a pure devotee of the Lord in a bona fide disciplic succession of spiritual masters stemming from Lord Kṛṣṇa Himself. Therefore, *Bhagavad-gītā As It Is* presents Lord Kṛṣṇa's message without the slightest distortion or personal interpretation. Thus it is the first edition to have actually awakened the dormant Kṛṣṇa consciousness of its readers.

3. The banyan is the sacred Indian fig tree (*Ficus bengalensis*). Its branches drop shoots to the ground, and these take root and support their parent branches. Extending itself in this way, one tree will often cover a very large area.

4. *Śrīmad-Bhāgavatam,* one of the eighteen *Purāṇas,* is generally known as "the spotless *Purāṇa.*" It was written down five thousand years ago by Śrīla Vyāsadeva, who specifically intended it for the people of the present dark age of hypocrisy and quarrel. It is the

original commentary on the *Vedānta-sūtra* (by the same author) and is the cream of all Vedic literatures. Here Śrīla Prabhupāda quotes a verse from the Second Canto of the *Bhāgavatam* (2.3.19). In Śrīla Prabhupāda's English rendering of the *Bhāgavatam,* this verse appears as follows:

श्वविड्वराहोष्ट्रखरैः संस्तुतः पुरुषः पशुः ।
न यत्कर्णपथोपेतो जातु नाम गदाग्रजः ॥

śva-viḍ-varāhoṣṭra-kharaiḥ
saṁstutaḥ puruṣaḥ paśuḥ
na yat-karṇa-pathopeto
jātu nāma gadāgrajaḥ

TRANSLATION: Men who are like dogs, hogs, camels and asses praise those men who never listen to the transcendental pastimes of Lord Śrī Kṛṣṇa, the deliverer from evils.

PURPORT: The general mass of people, unless they are trained systematically for a higher standard of life in spiritual values, are no better than animals, and in this verse they have particularly been put on the level of dogs, hogs, camels and asses. Modern university education practically prepares one to acquire a doggish mentality with which to accept the service of a greater master. After finishing a so-called education, the so-called educated persons move like dogs from door to door with applications for some service, and mostly they are driven away, informed of no vacancy. As dogs are negligible animals and serve the master faithfully for bits of bread, a man serves a master faithfully without sufficient rewards.

Persons who have no discrimination in the matter of foodstuff and who eat all sorts of rubbish are compared to hogs. Hogs are very much attached to eating stools. So stool is a kind of foodstuff for a particular type of animal. And even stones are eatables for a particular type of animal or bird. But the human being is not meant for eating everything and anything; he is meant to eat grains, vegetables, fruits, milk, sugar, etc. Animal food is not meant for the human being. For chewing solid food, the human being has a particular type of teeth meant for cutting fruits and vegetables. The human being is endowed with two canine teeth as a concession for persons who will eat animal food at any cost. It is known to everyone that one man's food is another man's poison. Human beings are expected to accept the remnants of food offered to Lord Śrī Kṛṣṇa, and the Lord accepts foodstuff from the categories of leaves, flowers, fruits, etc. (Bg. 9.26). As prescribed by Vedic scriptures, no animal food is offered to the Lord. Therefore, a human being is meant to eat a particular type of food. He should not imitate the animals to derive so-called vitamin values. Therefore, a person who has no discrimination in regard to eating is compared to a hog.

The camel is a kind of animal that takes pleasure in eating thorns. A person who wants to enjoy family life or the worldly life of so-called enjoyment is compared to the camel. Materialistic life is full of thorns, and so one should live only by the prescribed method of Vedic regulations just to make the best use of a bad bargain. Life in the material world is maintained by sucking one's own blood. The central point of attraction for material enjoyment is sex life. To enjoy sex life is to suck one's own blood, and there is not much more to be explained in this connection. The camel also sucks its own blood while chewing thorny twigs. The thorns the camel eats cut the tongue of the camel, and so blood begins to flow within the camel's mouth. The thorns, mixed with fresh blood, create a taste for the foolish camel, and so he enjoys the thorn-eating business with false pleasure. Similarly, the great business magnates, industrialists who work very hard to earn money by different ways and questionable means, eat the thorny results of their actions mixed with their own blood. Therefore the *Bhāgavatam* has situated these diseased fellows along with the camels.

The ass is an animal who is celebrated as the greatest fool, even among the animals. The ass works very hard and carries burdens of the maximum weight without making profit for itself. The ass is generally engaged by the washerman, whose social position is not very respectable. And the special qualification of the ass is that it is very much accustomed to being kicked by the opposite sex. When the ass begs for sexual intercourse, he is kicked by the fair sex, yet he still follows the female for such sexual pleasure. A henpecked man is compared, therefore, to the ass. The general mass of people work very hard, especially in the age of Kali. In this age the human being is actually engaged in the work of an ass, carrying heavy burdens and driving *ṭhelā* and rickshaws. The so-called advancement of human civilization has engaged a human being in the work of an ass. The laborers in great factories and workshops are also engaged in such burdensome work, and after working hard during the day, the poor laborer has to be again kicked by the fair sex, not only for sex enjoyment but also for so many household affairs.

So *Śrīmad-Bhāgavatam's* categorization of the common man without any spiritual enlightenment into the society of dogs, hogs, camels and asses is not at all an exaggeration. The leaders of such ignorant masses of people may feel very proud of being adored by such a number of dogs and hogs, but that is not very flattering. The *Bhāgavatam* openly declares that although a person may be a great leader of such dogs and hogs disguised as men, if he has no taste for being enlightened in the science of Kṛṣṇa, such a leader is also an animal and nothing more. He may be designated as a powerful, strong animal, or a big animal, but in the estimation of *Śrīmad-Bhāgavatam* he is never given a place in the category of man, on account of his atheistic temperament. Or, in other words, such godless leaders of dogs and hoglike men are bigger animals with the qualities of animals in greater proportion.

5. Sometimes a very hungry person will pick up a discarded piece of sugarcane, from which someone else has sucked out the sugary juice, and chew the already chewed pulp in an effort to get some sweet taste. This is called "chewing the chewed."

6. Śrīla Bhaktivinoda Ṭhākura (1838–1914) is one of the great *ācāryas,* or teachers of Kṛṣṇa consciousness in the succession of spiritual masters. His son, Śrīla Bhaktisiddhānta Sarasvatī Gosvāmī Mahārāja Prabhupāda, was the spiritual master of His Divine Grace A. C. Bhaktivedanta Swami Prabhupāda. Śrīla Bhaktivinoda Ṭhākura wrote prolifically on the science of Kṛṣṇa consciousness. In 1896 he initiated the teachings of Kṛṣṇa consciousness in the Western world by sending a copy of one of his small books—*Śrī Caitanya Mahāprabhu: His Life and Precepts*—to McGill University in Canada. Many of his Bengali songs are available in *Songs of the Vaiṣṇava Ācāryas,* published by the Bhaktivedanta Book Trust.

7. In the ascending process of investigation, a person attempts to realize the truth by personal observation followed by speculation. In the descending process, on the other hand, he accepts instructions from an authorized source. These two methods of inquiry are known as induction and deduction, respectively.

8. "My Guru Mahārāja" refers to Śrīla Prabhupāda's spiritual master, Śrīla Bhaktisiddhānta Sarasvatī Gosvāmī Mahārāja.

9. *Jagad-guru* means "*guru* of the entire world."

10. A Vaiṣṇava is a devotee of Lord Viṣṇu. Kṛṣṇa is the original form of Viṣṇu; therefore all the devotees of Kṛṣṇa are Vaiṣṇavas.

11. Raghunātha dāsa Gosvāmī was a contemporary and an exalted devotee of Śrī Kṛṣṇa Caitanya Mahāprabhu. He was one of the six Gosvāmīs entrusted with continuing Lord Caitanya's mission of spreading Kṛṣṇa consciousness throughout the world. Although born in a very wealthy family, Raghunātha dāsa Gosvāmī led a life of great austerity after he met Lord Caitanya.

12. *Bhagavad-gītā* 18.54. Lord Kṛṣṇa says, "One who is thus transcendentally situated at once realizes the Supreme Brahman and becomes fully joyful. He never laments nor desires to have anything; he is equally disposed to every living entity. In that state he attains pure devotional service unto Me."

13. *Karma* means "activity," and the law of *karma* refers to the process in which higher authorities award us favorable or unfavorable reactions according to our pious or impious activities, respectively. As the Bible says, "As ye sow, so shall ye reap." Thus, our present condition—whether we are wealthy, wise or beautiful, or whether we have an American, an Indian or a Japanese body—completely depends on the activities we performed in our previous life or lives.

Ultimately, all *karma,* whether good or bad, is unfavorable, for it binds us to the material world. Devotional service in Kṛṣṇa consciousness, however, is *akarmic.* In other words, it produces no reaction at all. Hence, when Arjuna killed his opponents on the Battlefield of Kurukṣetra, he suffered no reaction, for he was simply carrying out the will of Lord Kṛṣṇa.

14. DNA molecules are essential building and replicating units in organic cells. Many scientists regard them as the source of life, but according to Vedic science we must distinguish the chemical constituents of the body (such as DNA) from the very source of the life symptoms, which is the spirit soul.

15. Demigods are beings more advanced than humans. Although they resemble us, they possess far greater intelligence and beauty, wonderful mystic powers and, in some cases, many arms and heads. In the material universe there are thirty-three million administrative

demigods, each of whom is responsible for a particular phase of cosmic management (such as heat, light, water or air).

16. *Bhagavad-gītā* 6.41–42. "After many, many years of enjoyment on the planets of the pious living entities, the unsuccessful *yogī* is born into a family of righteous people, into a family of rich aristocracy, or into a family of transcendentalists, who are surely great in wisdom. Verily, such a birth is rare in this world."

17. *Bhagavad-gītā* 18.61. "The Supreme Lord is situated in everyone's heart, O Arjuna, and is directing the wanderings of all living entities, who are seated as on a machine made of the material energy."

18. Rādhārāṇī is the supreme devotee of Lord Kṛṣṇa, and She is His eternal consort. She is also considered to be the embodiment of Kṛṣṇa's internal, spiritual energy of pleasure.

19. The *brahmāstra* is a subtle nuclear weapon sometimes employed in the Vedic military art. It was released by the chanting of a *mantra,* and even if released from a long distance, it could annihilate any target, large or small, without harming anything else. For further information, see *Śrīmad-Bhāgavatam,* First Canto, Chapter Eight.

20. Vālmīki was a great Vedic sage and scholar. He wrote the *Rāmāyaṇa,* one of the most important histories in Vedic literature.

21. Lord Caitanya Mahāprabhu is described in Vaiṣṇava literature as the most merciful incarnation of God because He distributed love of Godhead freely, without consideration of one's caste, color or creed. He appeared in Bengal in 1486 and is also known as "the Golden Avatāra" because of His beautiful golden complexion. Lord Caitanya Mahāprabhu emphasized the chanting of the *mahā-mantra*—Hare Kṛṣṇa, Hare Kṛṣṇa, Kṛṣṇa Kṛṣṇa, Hare Hare/ Hare Rāma, Hare Rāma, Rāma Rāma, Hare Hare.

22. These four holy cities of India are hundreds of miles apart.

23. *Vai* means "without," and *kuṇṭha* means "anxiety." Thus in Vaikuṇṭha (the kingdom of God) there is no anxiety. The Vaikuṇṭha planets are in the spiritual realm, far beyond the material universes,

and everyone there lives in eternal bliss and knowledge, rendering devotional service to Lord Viṣṇu (Kṛṣṇa).

24. Forty thousand light-years equal over 235 quadrillion miles.

25. The *gopīs* are the cowherd girls of Vṛndāvana, and their absorption in Kṛṣṇa consciousness and love for Kṛṣṇa are unexcelled. However, one should never compare the loving affairs of Kṛṣṇa and the *gopīs,* which are completely transcendental, to mundane sexual affairs. While leading lives of celibacy and extreme austerity, Lord Caitanya and the six Gosvāmīs were constantly absorbed in the mood of the *gopīs.* Chief among the *gopīs* is Śrīmatī Rādhārāṇī.

26. Kaṁsa was the greatest demon of his time, and Kṛṣṇa's most persistent enemy as well. In *Kṛṣṇa, the Supreme Personality of Godhead* (a summary study of the Tenth Canto of *Śrīmad-Bhāgavatam*), Śrīla Prabhupāda tells how Kaṁsa tried many times to kill Kṛṣṇa. Finally, Kṛṣṇa killed Kaṁsa with His bare hands in the wrestling arena of Mathurā.

27. Pūtanā was a fearsome demoness sent by Kaṁsa to Vṛndāvana to kill Kṛṣṇa. She smeared deadly poison on her breast and offered it to baby Kṛṣṇa to suck. Kṛṣṇa, well aware of her intentions, sucked out her life air and killed her.

His Divine Grace A.C. Bhaktivedanta Swami Prabhupāda

His Divine Grace A. C. Bhaktivedanta Swami Prabhupāda appeared in this world in 1896 in Calcutta, India. He first met his spiritual master, Śrīla Bhaktisiddhānta Sarasvatī Gosvāmī, in Calcutta in 1922. Bhaktisiddhānta Sarasvatī, a prominent religious scholar and the founder of sixty-four Gauḍīya Maṭhas (Vedic institutes), liked this educated young man and convinced him to dedicate his life to teaching Vedic knowledge. Śrīla Prabhupāda became his student, and eleven years later (1933) at Allahabad he became his formally initiated disciple.

At their first meeting, in 1922, Śrīla Bhaktisiddhānta Sarasvatī Ṭhākura requested Śrīla Prabhupāda to broadcast Vedic knowledge through the English language. In the years that followed, Śrīla Prabhupāda wrote a commentary on the *Bhagavad-gītā,* assisted the Gauḍīya Maṭha in its work and, in 1944, without assistance, started an English fortnightly magazine, edited it, typed the manuscripts and checked the galley proofs. He even distributed the individual copies and struggled to maintain the publication. Once begun, the magazine never stopped; it is now being continued by his disciples in the West and is published in over twenty languages.

Recognizing Śrīla Prabhupāda's philosophical learning and devotion, the Gauḍīya Vaiṣṇava Society honored him in 1947 with the title "Bhaktivedanta." In 1950, at the age of fifty-four, Śrīla Prabhupāda retired from married life, adopting the *vānaprastha* (retired) order to devote more time to his studies and writing. Śrīla Prabhupāda traveled to the holy city of Vṛndāvana, where he lived in very humble circumstances in the historic medieval temple of Rādhā-Dāmodara. There he engaged for several years in deep study and writing. He accepted the renounced order of life (*sannyāsa*) in 1959. At Rādhā-Dāmodara, Śrīla Prabhupāda began work on his life's masterpiece: a multivolume translation of and commentary on the eighteen-thousand-verse *Śrīmad-Bhāgavatam*

(*Bhāgavata Purāṇa*). He also wrote *Easy Journey to Other Planets.*

After publishing three volumes of the *Bhāgavatam,* Śrīla Prabhupāda came to the United States, in 1965, to fulfill the mission of his spiritual master. Subsequently, His Divine Grace wrote more than sixty volumes of authoritative translations, commentaries and summary studies of the philosophical and religious classics of India.

In 1965, when he first arrived by freighter in New York City, Śrīla Prabhupāda was practically penniless. It was after almost a year of great difficulty that he established the International Society for Krishna Consciousness in July of 1966. Before his passing away on November 14, 1977, he guided the Society and saw it grow to a worldwide confederation of more than one hundred *āśramas,* schools, temples, institutes and farm communities.

In 1968, Śrīla Prabhupāda created New Vrindaban, an experimental Vedic community in the hills of West Virginia. Inspired by the success of New Vrindaban, now a thriving farm community of more than one thousand acres, his students have since founded several similar communities in the United States and abroad.

In 1972, His Divine Grace introduced the Vedic system of primary and secondary education in the West by founding the Gurukula school in Dallas, Texas. Since then, under his supervision, his disciples have established children's schools throughout the United States and the rest of the world. As of 1978, there are ten Gurukula schools worldwide, with the principal educational center now located in Vṛndāvana, India.

Śrīla Prabhupāda also inspired the construction of several large international cultural centers in India. The center at Śrīdhāma Māyāpur in West Bengal is the site for a planned spiritual city, an ambitious project for which construction will extend over the next decade. In Vṛndāvana, India, is the magnificent Kṛṣṇa-Balarāma Temple and International Guesthouse. There is also a major cultural and educational center in Bombay. Other centers are planned in a dozen other important locations on the Indian subcontinent.

Śrīla Prabhupāda's most significant contribution, however, is his books. Highly respected by the academic community for their authoritativeness, depth and clarity, they are used as standard textbooks in numerous college courses. His writings have been translated into over thirty languages. The Bhaktivedanta Book Trust, established in 1972 exclusively to publish the works of His Divine Grace, has thus become the world's largest publisher of books in the field of Indian religion and philosophy.

In just twelve years, in spite of his advanced age, Śrīla Prabhupāda circled the globe fourteen times on lecture tours that took him to six continents. In spite of such a vigorous schedule, Śrīla Prabhupāda continued to write prolifically. His writings constitute a veritable library of Vedic philosophy, religion, literature and culture.

The Challenge

Dr. Abraham T. Kovoor is president of the Sri Lanka branch of the Rationalist Association, an organization especially dedicated to disproving the existence of God and the soul. On August 14, 1977, the Colombo (Sri Lanka) *Sunday Times* published an article by Dr. Kovoor entitled "Is There Life After Death?" In this article, Dr. Kovoor maintained that life is merely a complex chemical activity and that the soul cannot survive death, since there is actually no such thing as the soul. This article led to a heated debate, both in the *Sunday Times* and in correspondence, between Dr. Kovoor and members of the Sri Lanka branch of the International Society for Krishna Consciousness. The *Sunday Times* articles and a portion of the correspondence are reproduced here.

Sunday Times
August 21, 1977

It's Beyond Kovoor's Power of Observation

[by Śrīla Haṁsadūta Svāmī and Mahākānta dāsa]

Although Dr. Kovoor and men of his stamp stand proudly on their platform of knowledge, it should be pointed out for the benefit of members of the public not expert in sophistry that men like Dr. Kovoor, who pose as the guardians of logic, reason and the advancement of science, are sailing on a sinking ship when they meddle in matters that lie beyond the purview of their limited senses. This particularly applies to the question of life after death.

The very first line of Dr. Kovoor's article is, "I do not hold the view that my life is located in a particular spot in my body." This statement, as well as a later one—"I do not believe that I have a soul or spirit to survive my death"—betrays the flimsy platform upon which he has chosen to make his stand. Throughout the article Dr. Kovoor gives his views, beliefs and opinions regarding a subject completely beyond his power of observation, and he tries to pass these imaginative speculations off as infallible scientific truths.

With all due respect to Dr. Kovoor, I beg to point out that the process of direct sensory perception, on the strength of which he has made so many statements regarding life after death, is completely limited and imperfect.

Consider, for example, the eyes. They function only under certain conditions: if there is no light, I cannot even see my hand in front of my face. We cannot see the nearest object to the eye—the eyelid—nor can we see that which is farthest away, the outer limits of the universe. Indeed, the eyes are imperfect. Similarly, the senses of touch, taste and smell are limited, and the mind, too, is imperfect. Therefore any conclusions based on imperfect sensory perception must necessarily be imperfect.

Research, experimentation and speculation conducted on the basis of imperfect sensory perception are meaningless when applied to matters that do not come within their purview. Attempting to apply sensory perception to such matters would be like a child's trying to find who his father is by asking every man in the world—a preposterous idea, to say the least. To understand the identity of one's father, one must accept the authority of one's mother—there is no other way. Since no one is able to see his father at the time of conception, one must accept the version of one's mother. Any sane man must accept this.

Regarding souls and rebirth, Dr. Kovoor writes, "I have not any valid reason or evidence to believe it." This statement only goes to show that the process of direct sensory perception is limited and imperfect and that it therefore yields no result when applied to matters beyond its jurisdiction. Rather than foolishly declaring, "I do not believe that I have a soul or spirit to survive my death," Dr. Kovoor would be much safer and more faithful to his professional ethic if he were simply to admit his inability or incompetence to deal with the subject matter in question. There is the soul, there is rebirth of the soul, and there is a Supreme

Soul—God. However, we should point out that because the soul is categorically different from matter, the techniques of material science must fail when applied to understanding the soul's existence and nature.

This does not mean, however, that the subject is open to the random speculation and opinion-making so fashionable today. Just as we have a material science to deal with material phenomena, so also we have a spiritual scientific process which allows its practitioner to penetrate the walls of gross and subtle matter and directly experience the truths of the soul, its rebirth, and its relationship with God, the Supreme Soul.

A true scientist would never prematurely declare, "I do not believe that I have a soul or spirit to survive my death." Rather, he would enthusiastically embrace a standard technique accepted by respected and recognized men of spiritual science. Such a scientist and sincere seeker of truth would then, in the interests of science, submit himself to that process and make himself the object of experimentation. Only after he had perfectly applied all the practices and techniques to himself, under the guidance of an authorized professor of spiritual science, would he dare make judgmental remarks about the subject in question. Theory, observation and experimentation are the true methods of science, and they apply equally to spiritual science.

Life is not generated from a combination of chemicals, as some scientists would have us believe. Rather, it is life which generates matter. A living man and a living woman combined in sexual intercourse are the cause for generating a living child. A dead man and a dead woman have no power to generate living offspring. A living tree has the power to generate fruit; a dead tree, however, has no such power. The difference between life and death is the soul, which is described in *Bhagavad-gītā* as superior energy (*parā prakṛti*). It is this superior energy which manifests all phenomena within our experience.

If life is a display of chemical combinations only, as some scientists suggest, why can't science inject a life-giving chemical into a dead body and make a man live forever? If we give a scientist the chemical ingredients of the material body, why can't he combine the chemicals and bring them to life?

When confronted with these questions, materialistic scientists will answer, "We are trying. We will do it in the future." But this is not science. This is a bluff.

These scientists proudly declare, "There is no soul. There is no God. Everything has come about by chance." But when asked to do something substantial to back up their claim, they can offer us only a postdated check: "We are trying. We shall do it in the future." Dr. Kovoor, being a typical materialistic scientist, resorts to this same bluff when he says, "The time will not be far off when man will be using his advanced knowledge in genetics to improve the quality of his own species."

Here is my challenge to Dr. Kovoor. Let him inject the appropriate chemicals into a dead body to bring it back to life. Or let him inject the appropriate chemicals into himself to check his own death and restore his old and worn-out body to its youthful luster and beauty.

If he finds this task too difficult, perhaps he could just produce a simple form of life, such as a mosquito or a bedbug. Better still, let him recombine the chemicals of the praying mantis he decapitated (as described in his article) and bring it back to life. Or is the science of Dr. Kovoor only a one-way road to the destruction of life?

It may be that science is not yet ready with a one-step process by which to produce life as a finished product. If this is so, let Dr. Kovoor merely make a plastic egg, inject it with yellow and white chemicals, incubate his artificial egg and thereby produce even one chicken that could go on laying eggs and producing more and more chickens.

Even this task may be a little too difficult for Dr. Kovoor. Perhaps, then, he could simply produce a drop of milk or a grain of rice by chemical combination. Then we could start taking him seriously.

Of course, everyone knows that these are impossible tasks for even the most powerful so-called scientist. Dr. Kovoor, in his next exposition, will undoubtedly give the reader a long-winded barrage of words to cover up his bluff. The sum and substance of it will be "We will do it in the future. We are trying." In any language, this is merely a bluff.

Haṁsadūta Svāmī
Mahākānta dāsa
International Society for Krishna Consciousness

Sunday Times
August 28, 1977

It's Not Beyond Kovoor's Power of Observation

[by Dr. Abraham Kovoor]

In the article titled "It's Beyond Kovoor's Power of Observation," in the *Sunday Times* of August 21, Messrs. Mahākānta dāsa and Haṁsadūta Svāmī of the "Hare Krishna" cult betray their appalling ignorance of modern branches of biological science such as biochemistry, molecular biology, neurobiology, eugenics, genetic engineering, extra-uterine insemination, parthenogenesis, and so on.

It is clear from what they have written that they are equating life with mind and the nonexisting spirit or soul. They do not seem to know that while all organisms have life, only those animals which possess nervous systems have mind, and that mental faculties in animals vary in direct proportion to the development of their nervous systems. Despite the beliefs of millions of religionists for thousands of years, there is absolutely no biological evidence for the existence of souls in organisms. Messrs. Dāsa and Svāmī say that according to the "professors of spiritual science," there is the soul, there is rebirth of the soul, and there is the Supreme Soul—God.

I should like to know on what objective evidence these so-called professors make this fantastic statement. According to the two writers, life is prior to matter. They say, "Life is not generated from a combination of chemicals, as some scientists would have us believe. Rather, it is life that generates matter."

The prime source of life on the planet earth is the sun. Solar energy is fixed in green plants when sunlight is converted into chemical energy by the reaction sequence known as photosynthesis. Organisms other than plants obtain their energy by eating green plants or some of the eaters of green plants. These food substances serve as fuel for supplying vital energy to organisms. The energy in the food is liberated as vital energy by slow oxidation during respiration.

Dāsa and Svāmī say that scientists, with their imperfect sensory powers, are incapable of understanding the reality of things as "spiritual scientists" do. Are the sensory powers of these pseudoscientists more efficient than those of real scientists? Or do the so-called spiritual scientists possess any form of perception other than sensory perception?

Knowledge and enlightenment cannot be had through meditation, which is only a form of self-hypnosis.

Dāsa and Svāmī ask whether scientists can make a chicken come out of a plastic egg.

I do not know whether they are aware that scientists have made over ten elements, such as fermium, plutonium and einsteinium, which God could not create because he did not know the technology involved in making them. Are these two men aware of the success of the Sri Lankan scientist Dr. Cyril Ponnamperuma and the Indian scientist Dr. Bal Gobind Khorana, the Nobel Prize winner, in synthesizing amino acids, the building blocks of living protoplasm, from inert substances, simulating conditions that prevailed in the primitive atmosphere of the earth? Do they know that human egg and sperm cells could be fertilized in test tubes, and the fetus developed in an artificial womb or in the womb of a hired woman?

Among animals that have evolved on this planet, man is the only animal that has progressed in all his activities. This he has achieved through his knowledge and science. While all organisms continue to live even today as their forebears did millions of years ago, man alone has progressed from the caveman state to the present spaceman state by using science and technology, and not by the help of any God or knowledge obtained from any scripture!

Advancements in medical science and social welfare services are helping more and more misfits survive to procreate more and more misfits as future citizens. While the short-term goal is achieved, the long-term goal is jeopardized. Future governments are not going to allow the misfits to procreate misfit children on the ground that "life originates from the Supreme Soul."

It is the unique ability of man to engage in creative thinking that has made him succeed in his fight against the laws of nature. The highly developed forebrain and the deeply convoluted cortex have helped him to think creatively. Scientists, as a general rule, are objective thinkers, because they base their thoughts on empirical knowledge. Mystics and visionaries, the so-called spiritual scientists of Dāsa and Svāmī, on the other hand, build up their thoughts on their subjective perceptions. Books on chemistry, physics, mathematics, geography, history, geology, anthropology, paleontology, engineering, medical science, astronomy, etc., are the products of objective thinkers. On the other hand, books like *Arabian Nights, Gulliver's Travels,* fairy stories, *Mahābhārata, Rāmāyaṇa,* the Bible, the Koran, *Pilgrim's Progress, Jātaka* stories, astrology, palmistry, numerology, theology, demonology, etc., are the products of subjective thinkers. While the former are factual, the latter are fictitious.

Some of the marvelous achievements of mankind in recent years have been the liberation of atomic energy, space flight, landing on the moon, organ transplantation, satellite communication, etc. All these were achieved through science. Mentally deranged intellectuals are capable of expatiating on their hallucinations and often become founders and preachers of diverse types of religious cults.

Dr. Abraham T. Kovoor

Sunday Times
September 4, 1977

The Challenge Still Stands

[by Śrīla Haṁsadūta Svāmī]

First of all, it should be noted that Dr. Kovoor has done exactly what I predicted in my last article he would do—namely, he has swamped the reader with a deluge of word jugglery in order to avoid the main issue, which is this: if life is generated by chance biochemical combinations, as some scientists claim, can the scientist Kovoor, given the proper chemicals, make the chemicals come to life?

Instead of answering this point, he has cleverly written, "Scientists have created over ten elements, such as fermium, plutonium and einsteinium."

But elements are a far cry from living beings. Dr. Kovoor says that Dr. Cyril Ponnamperuma and Dr. Bal Gobind Khorana, the Nobel Prize winner, have synthesized the building blocks of living protoplasm. If this is a fact, why hasn't Dr. Kovoor met the challenge by creating life with these building blocks? My challenge still stands.

As for incubating a baby in the test tube, this can be done only if you take the sperm and ovum of a *living man and woman.* In other words, the seed of life required to produce the baby in the test tube cannot be created by so-called scientists. What is their credit if they produce a baby in a test tube? God is already producing millions of babies daily in nature's test tube, the womb. On the other hand, scientists are killing thousands of babies in the womb by abortion and calling it "scientific advancement."

Dr. Kovoor's statement that scientists are "objective thinkers, because they base their thoughts on empirical knowledge" only goes to emphasize our point that the soul lies beyond the jurisdiction of the limited senses. Therefore, a completely different process of approach has to be adopted. The definition of *empirical* is "that which is based on observation and experiment." Observation and experiment are conducted with limited senses, and therefore the conclusions thus derived are naturally limited and imperfect. Thus, the soul and the existence of God are in fact quite beyond Dr. Kovoor's power of observation. Why should he be so obstinate? This is a commonsense point that anyone can understand.

Dr. Kovoor says, "It is the unique ability of man to engage in creative thinking that has made him succeed in his fight against the laws of nature." This is a preposterous claim that only a fool would make. Nature forces everyone to undergo old age, disease, and finally death. Even the world's most powerful conquerors are helplessly dragged off the stage of life by nature in the shape of all-devouring death. Will Dr. Kovoor be the first living being in history who will not die? That remains to be seen.

Finally, Dr. Kovoor says, "Some of the marvelous achievements of mankind in recent years have been the liberation of atomic energy, space flight, landing on the moon," etc. Everyone knows that the first thing scientists did after discovering atomic energy was to manufacture the atomic bomb and promptly drop it on Japan, thus annihilating tens of thousands of innocent victims in a flash. Marvelous, indeed.

At the expense of untold billions of dollars and years of research and hard labor, scientists have supposedly gone to the moon. Of course, all they have "brought back" is a few blurry photos, a handful of rocks and the revelation that the moon is barren. And now they want more money to go to Mars. What is so marvelous about this? It is complete lunacy. On our own planet earth, millions of people are without food, shelter and basic education. Scientists would be more credible if, instead of spending billions of dollars to bring rocks from the moon, they would spend the taxpayer's hard-earned money to improve his own lot on earth. Rocks are rocks, whether from China, from the moon or from Mars. Or is it that science can turn the rocks into bread and cheese by applying some chemicals?

Now, to get to the main point, Dr. Kovoor asks on what objective evidence we have made the fantastic statements that life and matter both come from life, that there is a soul, that there is rebirth of the soul and that there is a Supreme Soul, or God. It is said, "Fight fire with fire." Therefore, I may simply refer Dr. Kovoor to the authoritative, rational and thoroughly scientific findings of three researchers, all with doctorates, who are members of the Bhaktivedanta Institute. After examining the evidence they have presented,* one who is truly a rationalist should agree with their conclusion that life never comes from matter, but only from life.

Haṁsadūta Svāmī
ISKCON Sri Lanka

After the *Sunday Times* had printed this exchange of articles, the Hare Kṛṣṇa movement publicly challenged Dr. Kovoor to prove his statement that life originates from chance biochemical combinations. ISKCON publicly offered Dr. Kovoor five hundred thousand rupees (sixty thousand dollars) if he could create any form of life—a mouse, a cat, a mosquito or any other plainly visible creature—from inert chemicals. The *Sunday Times* ran this story:

"The high priest of Sri Lanka rationalists, Dr. Abraham T. Kovoor, who has been challenging people for decades to prove the existence of God, the soul and rebirth, is now on the receiving end.

"ISKCON (The International Society for Krishna Consciousness) has now challenged Dr. Kovoor to prove his contention that life originated from matter.

" 'We, the members of the Hare Kṛṣṇa movement, are openly challenging him to produce any form of life, even a mosquito, by mixing chemicals together. If he cannot substantiate his theory, he should remain silent forever,' say the ISKCON members.

"They will be waiting for Dr. Kovoor at the Ramakrishna Mission Hall on September 20, at 6:30 P.M. Admission will be free to the public."

---

*Bhaktivedanta Institute monograph number one: *What Is Matter and What Is Life?* Monograph two: *Demonstration by Information Theory That Life Cannot Arise From Matter.* Monograph three: *Consciousness and the Laws of Nature.*

While the issues were thus drawn in the press, Haṁsadūta Svāmī and Dr. Kovoor crossed swords on their own in a continuing exchange of letters. Part of that exchange is reproduced here.

Haṁsadūta Svāmī
ISKCON Sri Lanka
September 6, 1977

Dr. Abraham T. Kovoor
Sri Lanka Rationalist Association

Dear Dr. Kovoor,

I have further deliberated and have decided to write you a few more words on the existence of God, the soul and the rebirth of the soul. I trust they may be of interest to you.

The greatest disease in the minds of the scientists is that they do not believe that something is a fact unless it is proved by scientific experiments. When a scientist makes a statement and he supports that statement with scientific experiments, everyone is completely convinced, and no questions are asked. When we talk about the spirit soul to these scientists, their usual response is, "How can one detect the presence of the soul?" Because they have been conditioned to working with machines, they wonder whether the soul can be detected by scientific experiments. However, scientists have to agree that even in their own scientific realm there are many facts that cannot be proved by experiments. The fact is that the soul is there, but in order to understand its existence we have to accept knowledge from the right person—Śrī Kṛṣṇa (God) or His representative in disciplic succession, the spiritual master.

Everyone in the scientific community knows that mathematicians work with an imaginary number called "i," which is the square root of minus one ($\sqrt{-1}=i$). This number does not figure among the natural numbers (1,2,3, etc.). However, important branches of mathematics—for example, the theory of analytical functions—are based on this imaginary unit. Without the help of this branch of mathematics, various complex theories and problems cannot be solved. Thus the existence of this number cannot be denied; yet there is no experiment to prove it. In a similar manner, scientists in the field of statistical mechanics also utilize various conceptual models—ensembles, for example—to explain their theories and arguments. These are all beyond the realm of experimental science. If scientists are willing to accept these imaginary and conceptual models, what is the difficulty in accepting the perfect knowledge given by Lord Kṛṣṇa, the supreme scientist?

Another scientific theory that is beyond the limit of experimental science is Heisenberg's uncertainty principle. The statement of this principle is that it is impossible to simultaneously determine the position and momentum of any object. In mathematical language, it is stated that the product of the uncertainties in the measured values of the position and momentum (product of mass and velocity) cannot be smaller than Planck's constant. No existing experimental technique can prove this principle. However, scientists all over the world accept this statement as a fact, knowing that the experimental proof is beyond their ability. Similarly, there is no scientific experiment to prove the Third Law of Thermodynamics. This law, as formulated by Planck, states that the entropy of a perfect crystal at absolute zero degrees is equal to zero. Factually, there is no way to directly measure the absolute entropies. Therefore the proof of this law is beyond the realm of experimental science.

It is also to be noted that so-called scientific theories are changing constantly. For example, at the beginning of the nineteenth century (1808), John Dalton, in developing his atomic theory, stated that atoms could not be further divided. However, toward the end of the nineteenth century and the beginning of the twentieth century, it was found that Dalton's atomic theory could no longer be considered correct. It was observed that atoms could be further divided into fundamental particles like electrons, protons and neutrons. It was also found that some atoms could emit alpha and beta particles, thereby producing new atoms, and so on. As a matter of fact, the so-called nuclear bombs are a result of these findings. In a similar manner, during the eighteenth and nineteenth centuries Newton's mechanics had a tremendous influence on the minds of scientists, since they could be applied to gross material objects. However, at the beginning of the twentieth century, with the discoveries of the fundamental particles, it was realized that Newton's mechanics failed in describing the motions of these particles. Thus quantum mechanics has been developed to explain the phenomena they exhibit. These theories are filled with speculation, and they are also changing. Just as past and present scientific theories are changing, so we can understand that future scientific theories will also change.

All of this simply shows that the brains of the highly honored scientists are imperfect, and as a result the theories proposed by these brains will always remain imperfect. Actually, perfect knowledge cannot be changed, but in order to get perfect knowledge one has to approach a perfect source. That source is Kṛṣṇa and the Vedic literature. Of course, this may seem like an incredible statement to a scientific brain like yours, which is accustomed to testing everything with scientific instruments and so-called logic, reason, deduction, hypothesis and theory, but it is nonetheless a fact. This can be understood by anyone who is scientific enough to experiment on himself by following the practices recommended in the *Vedas,* under the guidance of a self-realized soul.

The process is actually very practical. The spiritual master prescribes the process of spiritual discipline, and the student carries it out according to the directions given. If the student experiences the predicted result, then he concludes that the spiritual master was right. If the spiritual master is actually bona fide, the result will be positive. This procedure is quite similar to an honest scientist's reporting his results along with his experimental method. One who wants to verify the result can perform the same experiment himself. When the same result is reproduced by several scientists, it is accepted as a scientific fact.

In conclusion, I would like to point out that when someone believes that life comes from matter rather than from spirit, his concern for morality diminishes considerably. If all life is merely a complex combination of chance chemical reactions, and if there is no supreme consciousness, no creator and controller, what need is there for moral restraint? This is not a new philosophy. In ancient Greece, Epicurus postulated that everything is simply a combination of atoms and void, nothing more. Today the word "epicure" describes a person whose main activity is to enjoy fine food and drink. The conclusion is that the philosophy that chance biochemical combinations are the origin of life is a philosophy that leads to unrestricted sense gratification, but it is by no means scientific. We can see one vivid example of how demoralizing and vicious this philosophy is in the present worldwide practice of abortion. Because of being taught that the embryo is not actually a living being but only a mass of inanimate chemicals, people have been convinced to kill their unborn children mercilessly within the womb.

I will be very interested in receiving your thoughts on these points and am prepared to discuss the matter further if you have any doubts about them.

I hope this letter meets you well.

Respectfully yours,
Haṁsadūta Svāmī

Dr. Abraham T. Kovoor
Sri Lanka Rationalist Association
September 10, 1977

Mr. Haṁsadūta Svāmī
ISKCON Sri Lanka

Dear Sir:

From [your] letters it is clear that it is futile for me, who base my philosophy on available scientific evidence, and you, who base your faith on dubious scriptures called *Vedas,* to try to convince each other.

If you insist that I should substantiate, by a demonstration before the public eye, my view that life originated from inert substances by chemical evolution under suitable conditions, I too have an equal right to ask you to substantiate your statement that "whatever we see in existence is the creation of the Lord, and that creation is going on at every moment" by demonstrating it before the public eye. As long as you are not going to get your "Lord" to demonstrate this, you need not expect me to conduct a onesided show.

As far as I am concerned, the universe is only matter and energy in time and space. The question of a creator does not come in, because matter, energy, space and time have neither beginning nor end. The various forms of terrestrial organisms, extinct as well as extant, are the products of millions of years of biological evolution of macromolecules of protein that were formed on earth as a result of chemical evolution under suitable conditions.

Can you tell me who created your "Lord," and where he was before the universe was created?

Yours in search of truth,
Dr. Abraham T. Kovoor

Haṁsadūta Svāmī
ISKCON Sri Lanka
September 15, 1977

Dr. Abraham T. Kovoor
Sri Lanka Rationalist Association

Dear Dr. Kovoor,

I am in due receipt of your letter dated September 10, 1977, and have noted the contents carefully.

If it is futile to try to convince each other of our respective points of view, then what is the meaning of your science, rationalism and search for truth? The close of your letter—"Yours in search of truth"—suggests that you have not yet found the truth. That is your defect: you have not yet found truth, yet you pose and speak as if you were in knowledge of truth.

The first aphorism of the *Vedānta-sūtra* is *athāto brahma-jijñāsā:* "In the human form of life, one should inquire about the

Absolute Truth, or God." You do not know what God is, yet still you have written, "The question of the creator does not come in . . . The various forms of terrestrial organisms, extinct as well as extant, are products of millions of years of biological evolution of macromolecules of protein that were formed on earth as a result of chemical evolution under suitable circumstances." In simple English, you mean to say that life is a result of chance biochemical combinations. So if this is a fact—and if by this statement you wish to establish your credibility as a rationalist, scientist and seeker of truth—then why do you repeatedly fail to combine some chemicals and bring them to life, as I have challenged you so many times to do?

You say your philosophy is based on "existing scientific evidence." So where is the scientific evidence that life comes from chemicals? Mix the chemicals and prove it! You say, "As far as I am concerned, the universe is only matter and energy in time and space." Where did this matter and energy and time and space come from? Without giving any reason or evidence, you state, "The question of a creator does not come in, because matter, energy, time and space have neither beginning nor end." Then again you ask me, "Who created your 'Lord,' and where was he before the universe was created?" Your statements are inconsistent. First you say that matter, energy, time and space have neither beginning nor end, and then you ask where the Lord was before the creation of the universe. This is clearly contradictory. This shows that you still have a long way to go in your search for truth.

Research reaches its conclusion when one accepts knowledge from the *Vedas*. Indeed, *Vedānta* means "the end of knowledge."

Instead of providing evidence to support your fantastic statements, you try to cloud the real issue by counterchallenging God to create life. This kind of tactic is like that of a penniless beggar who, when brought before the judge to show his means of income, challenges the government to show its source of income first. Such a challenge would hardly be entertained.

According to Roman, Greek, British, American or international law, the burden of proof lies with the plaintiff, he who accuses, not with the defendant. You accuse the *Vedas* of being dubious, God of being fictitious and those who follow God and the *Vedas* of being mentally deranged, foolish, gullible, dogmatic fanatics. But the burden of proof is on you. Without giving reason or evidence, you say, "The question of a creator does not come in . . . everything is a matter of chance biochemical combination." Do I have to accept this blindly? The onus is on you. Mix the chemicals and produce life. That is science. But no scientist can create even an insignificant mosquito from chemicals. Therefore, under the circumstances, it appears that it is you, and not we, who may be mentally deranged, foolish, gullible, dogmatic and totally fanatic.

Scientists like to discredit the *Vedas* by saying that they are the writings of superstitious aborigines. But what kind of aborigines were they who wrote in a language so perfect in grammar, composition, poetry and meter that a scholar needs twelve years to master the grammar alone? What kind of aborigines were they who thousands of years ago formulated divisions of time beginning with one ten-thousandth of a second up to the complete duration of universal time? What kind of aborigines were they who could describe, thousands of years ago, all the planets that modern scientists have only recently discovered? Where is the scientist today who can perfectly describe the process of conception taking place in the womb, as the Vedic so-called aborigines did thousands of years ago? How could these uncivilized aborigines categorize and enumerate in the *Vedas* all the different species of life, numbering 8,400,000? How is it that the *Vedas,* which are supposed to be the dubious writings of uncivilized aborigines, contain systematic information on subjects such as music, medicine, art, politics, architecture, warfare and psychology? How could uncivilized aborigines even know the arts of reading and writing, much less describe the atom and atomic energy? How could they give descriptions of the orbits of the planets, their size, their eclipses and the size of the universe, and how could they describe the soul and the Supersoul, God?

If Kṛṣṇa is the Hindu aboriginal God, why did such a scientist as Oppenheimer pay Him heed by studying the *Bhagavad-gītā* spoken by Him? Why did Einstein, Schopenhauer, Kant, Hegel,

Emerson, Thoreau, Schweitzer and scores of scientists more important and brilliant than you read Vedic literature—especially *Bhagavad-gītā*—if these are books full of superstitions and the deranged ideas of uncivilized aborigines? What is your authority? Are you greater than God? Do you think that these highly learned and honored men were all fools and rascals who had nothing better to do than spend their valuable time reading the writings of uncivilized aborigines? Or could it be that the *Vedas* are books of knowledge originally given by God at the beginning of the creation, and that they are preserved by being handed down in a Vedic tradition of disciplic succession about which you unfortunately know nothing?

As a scientist, you would do well to take out some time and sincerely examine the *Vedas* on their own merit, not in terms of preconceived notions resulting from limited, imperfect speculations and experiments.

Whether one speaks for or against the existence of God, the central point is God. You say, "I hope you understand that it is not the way with science to provide proof for things that do not exist." But we see that the so-called scientist is very busy trying to prove the nonexistence of God. If God has no existence, why bother about Him? According to logic, one cannot conceive of a thing that does not exist. And if a nonexistent entity is inconceivable, where is the question of even discussing it, whether positively or negatively?

It is the peculiar madness of many so-called scientists that they cannot seem to get off the subject of God, who according to them has no existence. We see that the whole aim of their scientific research is to justify their rebellion against the authority of God and the scriptures by trying to find an alternative cause and reason for life and creation. Although these scientists would like to believe that life originated from inert chemicals, no one has ever observed such an event. Therefore, a science based on such beliefs can only be a science of rascals and fools.

My challenge to you, or to any scientist who claims that life originates from chemicals, still stands: mix the chemicals and produce life. Why can't you do it? You say, "It is like this. It is like that," so then why can't you produce life? Sunshine is available, the earth is present, the water, air, fire and all other ingredients are present, and life is being produced by God. If you are greater than God, why can't you produce something? What is the use of your talk if you cannot produce life? Nor can you stop old age, disease or death. Your talk is simply empty nonsense. You cannot do anything, yet still you are talking, saying that life comes from chemicals. You are a talking scientist, and I am a practical scientist. Take some chemicals and save yourself from old age, disease and death. I asked you to produce an egg—where is it? The chicken is a better scientist than you, because it lays an egg and within a month produces another chicken. Therefore you are less important than a chicken. Chickens are producing life, but you cannot produce anything but empty sounds.

In the service of Kṛṣṇa,
Haṁsadūta Svāmī

Having been challenged to demonstrate that he could create life at a public meeting, Dr. Kovoor declined to attend, saying that he would not feel obliged to demonstrate that he could create life unless God Himself were to appear in person to demonstrate the same thing. The *Times* reported this with the headline "Flummoxed Kovoor Passes the Buck." Then Śrīla Haṁsadūta Svāmī sent Dr. Kovoor this final letter.

Haṁsadūta Svāmī
ISKCON Sri Lanka
September 21, 1977

Dr. Abraham T. Kovoor
Sri Lanka Rationalist Association

Dear Dr. Kovoor,

You wanted to place yourself above God, but God's devotees defeated you, as the newspaper correctly noted. I'm sure that the readers were also enlightened regarding the theory that life comes from chemicals.

You may be interested to know that you are the first so-called scientist in the world to be officially challenged by ISKCON, and you are also the first to be totally exposed in the public press. Your case is a landmark in history. Because the spiritual life in most religious communities has long ago died out, practically no one has been able to properly put forward the theistic point of view in the modern age. The International Society for Krishna Consciousness, however, is presenting the *yuga-dharma,* the truly scientific method of religion for this age: it is perfectly teaching and following the Vedic religion. Of course, every religious movement claims to be genuine, but we have to distinguish the genuine from the fraudulent. Your defect is that because you have been repeatedly frustrated by encountering spiritual frauds, you have prematurely concluded that all religions are bogus. You want to brand God and religion fraudulent, but fraud can be understood only in relation to its genuine counterpart. That you fail to know. You do not know what is genuine.

I don't say that all scientists are frauds, but I do say that you or anyone claiming that life is generated from inert matter is definitely a fool or a fraud. In fact, you are both—because you obstinately cling to the foolish notion that life comes from chemicals. What is the difference between your theory and that of the alchemists, who attempted (and failed) to produce gold from chemicals? A modern scientist scoffs at the alchemists—yet he proposes to create life from chemicals. Isn't this the height of folly? I'm still open to be convinced that life comes from chemicals, if you can provide evidence by creating life from chemicals.

Now your life is nearly at an end, and at the time of death, when the messengers of death come for your soul, perhaps you will remember all this and understand everything. But then it will be too late, for you will be helplessly dragged off to repeat another life of material struggle in the shape of birth, death, old age and disease. But if one simply chants Hare Kṛṣṇa, he can be saved from this great struggle. I hope you will do that.

Haṁsadūta Svāmī

From the start of his Kṛṣṇa conscious career eleven years ago, Śrīla Haṁsadūta dāsa Svāmī has shown his fiery missionary spirit. After joining ISKCON in New York City, he helped establish centers in Montreal, Boston, Vancouver and Berkeley. In 1969, Śrīla Prabhupāda asked him to go to Germany, and for five years he traveled throughout that country, teaching the science of Kṛṣṇa consciousness, opening centers and overseeing the German translation and publication of Śrīla Prabhupāda's Bhagavad-gītā As It Is, Śrīmad-Bhāgavatam, Teachings of Lord Caitanya and other books. In 1976 Śrīla Prabhupāda gave him the renounced (sannyāsa) order, and today, as a member of the Governing Body Commission, a trustee of the Bhaktivedanta Book Trust and a Vaiṣṇava ācārya, Śrīla Haṁsadūta dāsa Svāmī directs ISKCON's activities in Sri Lanka (Ceylon) and Northwest U.S.A. and spreads Kṛṣṇa consciousness throughout South India.

(Editor's note: Dr. Abraham T. Kovoor died on September 18, 1978, in Sri Lanka. Although he was battling with cancer, the cause of death was determined to be heart failure.)

References

Bhagavad-gītā, 5, 8, 11, 14, 17, 20, 22, 24, 27, 30, 33, 38, 40, 45, 47, 49, 50, 51, 56, 57, 58, 59, 62, 63, 77, 81, 82, 84, 85, 86, 91, 98, 102

Brahma-saṁhitā, 41, 97, 100

Chāndogya Upaniṣad, 12

Īśopaniṣad, 15, 16, 100

Kaṭha Upaniṣad, 3

Śrīmad-Bhāgavatam, 10, 17, 19, 20, 101

Śvetāśvatara Upaniṣad, 28

Guide to Sanskrit Pronunciation

Throughout the centuries, the Sanskrit language has been written in a variety of alphabets. The mode of writing most widely used throughout India, however, is called *devanāgarī,* which means, literally, the writing used in "the cities of the demigods." The *devanāgarī* alphabet consists of forty-eight characters, including thirteen vowels and thirty-five consonants. Ancient Sanskrit grammarians arranged the alphabet according to practical linguistic principles, and this order has been accepted by all Western scholars. The system of transliteration used in this book conforms to a system that scholars in the last fifty years have accepted to indicate the pronunciation of each Sanskrit sound.

The short vowel **a** is pronounced like the **u** in b**u**t, long **ā** like the **a** in f**a**r and short **i** like the **i** in p**i**n. Long **ī** is pronounced as in p**i**que, short **u** as in p**u**ll and long **ū** as in r**u**le. The vowel **ṛ** is pronounced like the **ri** in **ri**m. The vowel **e** is pronounced as in th**e**y, **ai** as in **ai**sle, **o** as in g**o**, and **au** as in h**ow**. The *anusvāra* (**ṁ**), which is a pure nasal, is pronounced like the **n** in the French word *bo***n**, and *visarga* (**ḥ**), which is a strong aspirate, is pronounced as a final **h** sound. Thus **aḥ** is pronounced like **aha,** and **iḥ** like **ihi**.

The guttural consonants—**k, kh, g, gh** and **ṅ**—are pronounced from the throat, in much the same manner as in English. **K** is pronounced as in **k**ite, **kh** as in Ec**kh**art, **g** as in **g**ive, **gh** as in di**g-h**ard, and **ṅ** as in si**ng.** The palatal consonants—**c, ch, j, jh** and **ñ**—are pronounced from the palate with the middle of the tongue. **C** is pronounced as in **ch**air, **ch** as in staun**ch-h**eart, **j** as in **j**oy, **jh** as in he**dgeh**og, and **ñ** as in ca**ny**on. The cerebral consonants—**ṭ, ṭh, ḍ, ḍh** and **ṇ**—are pronounced with the tip of the tongue turned up and drawn back against the dome of the palate. **Ṭ** is pronounced as in **t**ub, **ṭh** as in ligh**t-h**eart, **ḍ** as in **d**ove, **ḍh** as in re**d-h**ot, and **ṇ** as in **n**ut. The dental consonants—**t, th, d, dh** and **n**—are pronounced in the same manner as the cerebrals, but with the forepart of the tongue against the teeth. The labial consonants—**p, ph, b, bh** and **m**—are pronounced with the lips. **P** is pronounced as in **p**ine, **ph** as in u**ph**ill, **b** as in **b**ird, **bh** as in ru**b-h**ard, and **m** as in **m**other. The semivowels—**y**, **r**, **l** and **v**—are pronounced as in **y**es, **r**un, **l**ight and **v**ine respectively. The sibilants—**ś**, **ṣ** and **s**—are pronounced, respectively, as in the German word **s**prechen and the English words **sh**ine and **s**un. The letter **h** is pronounced as in **h**ome.

Keep in Touch...

Please send me a free information package including the small booklet *Krishna, the Reservoir of Pleasure,* and a catalogue of books available.

Name ______________________________

Address ____________________________

____

State _______________ Post Code _____

Return this coupon to:
The Bhaktivedanta Book Trust,
P.O. Box 262 Botany, NSW 2019, Australia

The Bhaktivedanta Book Trust
P.O. Box 324, Borehamwood, Herts. WD6 1NB,
United Kingdom

The Bhaktivedanta Book Trust
3764 Watseka Ave
Los Angeles Ca 90034
U.S.A.

The Bhaktivedanta Book Trust
P.O. Box 56003, Chatsworth Circle, Chatsworth 4020
Durban, South Africa